# THE YOUTH MINISTRY SURVIVAL GUIDE

## HOW TO THRIVE AND LAST FOR THE LONG HAUL

## by Len Kage

 ZONDERVAN®

ZONDERVAN.com/
AUTHORTRACKER
follow your favorite authors

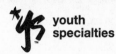 youth
specialties

**youth
specialties**

*The Youth Ministry Survival Guide: How to Thrive and Last for the Long Haul*
Copyright 2008 by Len Kageler

Youth Specialties resources, 300 S. Pierce St., El Cajon, CA 92020 are published by Zondervan, 5300 Patterson Ave. SE, Grand Rapids, MI 49530.

ISBN 978-0-310-27663-0

*Cover design by SharpSeven Design*
*Interior design by Mark Novelli, IMAGO MEDIA*

*Printed in the United States of America*

08  09  10  11  12  13  •  20  19  18  17  16  15  14  13  12  11  10  9  8  7  6  5  4  3  2  1

# CONTENTS

# FOREWORD

## BY DUFFY ROBBINS

We've all seen those little charts labeled "Troubleshooting Guide."

If you buy a new camera, you'll find the troubleshooting guide placed discreetly at the back of the instruction manual as if it were simply an afterthought, little more than an unnecessary extravagance, an add-on for tech geeks who have already read all their other camera and software guides but would still like one more time to read the word *simply*... followed by lines of indiscernible technological gibberish before they log off for another day. Tucked away at the very end of the book, these guides seem to suggest: "Of course, this is information you'll never need. We don't even know why we put this stuff in here. In fact, we're a little embarrassed to have it in the book. After all, what could possibly go wrong? But, if you're curious, here it is..."

And then, of course, there are the actual instructions themselves:

*Problem:*      *No image in viewfinder.*

*Solution:*      *Remove lens cap.*

*Problem:*      *Viewfinder is showing image of lens cap.*

*Solution:*      *Aim camera away from where you placed lens cap after you removed it.*

*Problem:*      *Image in viewfinder is blurry and flesh-toned.*

| | |
|---|---|
| *Solution:* | *Move finger slightly down and to the left, away from viewfinder.* |
| *Problem:* | *No message lights flashing to indicate camera has malfunctioned.* |
| *Solution:* | *Turn power button on. Malfunction lights should begin flashing immediately.* |

If you've ever meditated on this troubleshooting material in a late-night moment of quiet reflection and mouth-foaming rage, you have realized three fundamental facts about these guides:

1. Lots of stuff can go wrong.

2. The stuff that goes wrong is usually stuff the guide has conveniently neglected to mention.

3. When the problem *is* mentioned, both problem and solution are written in language that is completely unhelpful to real people out in the field.

Now, imagine a book that is nothing but a really effective troubleshooting guide. The suggestions aren't hidden in the back in a section marked "For Those Who Are Naive, in Serious Denial, or Have the Capabilities of a Lower Primate." It isn't written in language so complex that you need a whole other Instruction Guide just to understand it. And it warns you—in clear, real-life terms—about some of the possible issues you might face and how you can deal with them effectively.

The book you hold in your hands, *The Youth Ministry Survival Guide* by Len Kageler, is exactly that kind of book for youth workers. It's a book that promises, "A lot of stuff can go right—but don't kid yourself: A lot of stuff can definitely go wrong." It's a book that speaks with unblushing honesty about the everyday temptations and inconvenient realities we face as youth workers. And it's a book that offers both the description and the prescription in clear, practical, real-life terms that can help all of us in the trenches of everyday ministry.

Best of all, it's written by a guy who knows well both the equipment and the technique of effective youth ministry. Len Kageler is a college professor—widely respected in the circles of academic youth ministry—but he's no geek. Len's many years of hands-on youth ministry experience as a paid youth pastor, volunteer, and youth ministry trainer have given him lots of real-world experience in facing the trouble spots, dangers, and pitfalls of everyday youth ministry. His heart and his consistent faithful witness over the years remind us that Len Kageler is a guy who has more than a camera and a viewfinder—he has vision.

In the world of youth ministry today there are several notorious items on the troubleshooting chart—issues that cause the picture to turn out badly or at least not as good as we'd expected. In their extensive research of almost 2500 youth workers, Strommen, Jones, and Rahn identified six common concerns on the minds of youth workers—issues these researchers have labeled "six perils that can sink a career":

1. Feelings of personal inadequacy

2. Strained family relationships

3. A growing loss of confidence

4. Feeling unqualified for the job

5. Disorganized in one's work habits

6. Burnout

As if all that weren't enough to bring us a chart full of trouble, spiritual director and retreat leader Beth Slevcove reminds us that beneath these issues are often troubles of the soul—perils that spring from an inner deterioration of spirit:

- Instead of nurturing a spiritual intimacy, many youth workers display a compulsiveness to do more, work harder, and be better. Exhaustion and despair are inevitably the result.

- Often there is little or no awareness that intimacy with Christ, a sense of being deeply loved, a lasting peace, and the fruits that come from communion with him are even possible.

- Many lack a safe place to wrestle with issues, a safe person to be honest and accountable with (preferably outside of the church in which they are ministering).

- Often there is a belief that they should be a strong enough Christian to do it on their own and that sharing or asking for help is weakness.

- Many fail to see that God provides other members of the body of Christ to assist and companion each of us in our journeys of faith.

- Most have little sense of the importance of the concept of Sabbath—that constant productivity is not required of us, but resting in God is.

- Many carry the false belief that "What I do = Who I am." Thus, their sense of self-worth is often deeply wed to their job, which results in a need to be liked, praised, popular, and successful.

- Many are striving to live up to the stereotypical fun, charismatic, extroverted, cool youth worker, instead of recognizing their own giftedness and ministering in their own unique ways.

What I appreciate about *The Youth Ministry Survival Guide* is that it addresses, in one way or another, almost all of these problems, and it addresses them with just the right blend of faithful optimism, unblinking realism, and biblical wisdom. Of course, ultimately, we don't just want to know what can go wrong in youth ministry; we want to know how to make it right, or better yet, how to avoid the problems to begin with. That is another strength of this book. From Kageler's description of the four ways rookie youth workers sometimes get blindsided to his practical look at the "recipes for burnout" we often cook up as veteran youth workers, there is help in these pages for youth workers at all levels of ministry experience.

One word of warning before you begin to read: Don't turn away from some of the hard stuff in these pages. A book like this one forces us to look at ourselves in the mirror, and some of the tough issues we must face there can make us second-guess God's calling. Thinking through these kinds of questions can be like going to the doctor for a physical—we know we're going to have to step on the scales, we're going to experience what might be some awkward moments of exposure, and we may even feel a little pain. But we keep the appointment because we understand the value of good health. Maintaining a lifestyle of healthy leadership requires that we consider the tough issues in this book. The fact that some of these issues make us feel uncomfortable is not an altogether bad sign.

My hope is that you will honestly and prayerfully consider the danger areas and troubling questions posed by this book, and that you will be helped by its practical suggestions and encouraging wisdom. Most of all, I pray that, if you are going through one of those trouble spots, wondering if indeed you will be able to survive it, that you will remember two things. First, remember that God's best pictures are only fully developed through time in a darkroom of trial. Second, remember that the only way to bring clarity to the picture is through exposure to the Light.

Enjoy the book!

Duffy Robbins
Eastern University, St. Davids, Pennsylvania

# PREFACE

I've always wondered why some people in youth ministry seem to thrive and flourish, while others burn out or get pushed out.

I've been in some kind of paid or volunteer youth ministry since 1969, which, even to me, seems like a long time ago. In these years I've seen many of my friends and colleagues flourish, overcome obstacles, and embody the presence of Jesus among youth. I've seen churches so pleased and grateful for authentic youth ministry that they have been tempted to hoist the youth pastor to their shoulders and sing "Hosanna." On the other hand, I've seen all too many youth workers crash and burn. I've seen churches, after the (forced or otherwise) departure of their youth pastor vow "never again" when it comes to having a youth pastor as part of the pastoral staff.

The book in front of you is an extreme makeover of *The Youth Minister's Survival Guide* that I wrote in 1991. At the heart of the original book was a study I'd done of more than 100 youth pastors who had been fired from their positions. Youth Specialties approached me recently with the question of whether the reasons youth ministers get fired are still the same. They also asked me to address the issue of burnout in youth ministry.

This new edition of *The Youth Ministry Survival Guide* is grounded in a research survey conducted in the fall of 2006. Youth pastors were invited to respond to the survey if they'd ever been fired from a ministry position or left because of burnout *or* if they were close to someone who'd had this experience. (The survey was anonymous, but I included some identifiers so I could eliminate duplicate responses. Of the 373 responses, less than 1 percent were duplicates.) Any statistic you see in the text that is not footnoted comes from this survey. Though some names and details have been changed to protect anonymity, all the examples and stories you'll read are real (including my own—I have made some spectacular errors as a youth worker!)

Without tipping my hand as to what's coming, I know some things about youth ministry have changed since 1991.

While the field of youth ministry was once dominated by suburban churches, youth ministry today is much more urban. When the Billy Graham crusade came to New York City several summers ago, they held a breakfast for youth pastors. I wasn't able to attend (I live just outside the city), but my friends were pleased to say *more than 600* youth pastors and volunteers attended.

Youth ministry is also much more global than in 1991. There are youth pastors and youth ministry degree programs on every continent except Antarctica. And the joys/frustrations are similar everywhere. For example, among the "joys" cited by youth pastors in our survey were "seeing kids 'get it,'" "spending time with youth," and "worshipping with youth." These joys might well have come from pastors in Kansas, California, or Tennessee, but in reality they came from youth pastors in Nigeria, Hong Kong, and Peru. The writers were not North Americans doing youth ministry internationally—they are local youth pastors, all with youth ministry degrees or the equivalent.

How about the frustrations of youth ministry? Youth pastors in our survey were discouraged by "kids dropping out of church after age 18," "church bureaucracy," and "lack of money." Those words come from youth workers in New Zealand, the Netherlands, and South Africa.

Another big change is that youth ministry is no longer almost exclusively a Protestant endeavor. Catholic churches have gotten on board with youth ministry in a big way. The mission or vision statements of many Catholic youth ministries would be hard to distinguish from those of the Southern Baptists. In this new *Youth Ministry Survival Guide* you'll hear the voices of many urban, international, and Roman Catholic youth pastors in addition to the suburban or rural Protestant youth pastors.

My own experience in youth ministry has also changed since 1991. My career shifted in 1994 when I left my full-time job as a youth pastor, became a volunteer in youth ministry, and began teaching youth ministry at the college level. A Ph.D. in sociology has broadened my horizons, particularly related to the academic research that deepens our understanding of youth, youth groups, and youth work. But my youth ministry students know (and appreciate) that I still stand with wiggly and sometimes uncooperative junior highers every Wednesday night. My boss—the youth pastor at the church where I serve—is one of my former students. When he says "jump," my job is to ask, "How high?!" Recently in youth group an opening game was to mummy wrap (many rolls of TP to make the person appear as a mummy) one person from each team. I was chosen to be the mummy and was able to mumble encouragement and advice (they did my head first) from years of experience as being both the wrapper and wrappee.

Ultimately, my desire is this book would offer you help and support. I want the specific content to be something you can use practically. Just as important, I trust this will be a book of hope as well. By necessity, some of what we will talk about will be difficult, even painful. But I aim to lift our eyes beyond the "issues" and "crises" some experience in youth ministry to the One who is able to do—in, through, and around us—"immeasurably more than we could ever ask or imagine" (Ephesians 3:20).

# PART ONE

# GOOD TIMES AND HARD TIMES AHEAD

# CHAPTER 1

# YOUTH MINISTRY: WORTH THE EFFORT

Tim looked up from his chocolate chip muffin and, after a long pause, finally said to me, "I'll try to learn from this, but it sure is hard."

The church board, without the knowledge of the senior pastor, had met and decided to fire him. Tim had been there 12 months and had taken the church's fledgling youth group from just a handful to about 30 regular attendees. There was enthusiasm among the youth and the parents in this suburban California church for what had become a dynamic youth ministry. There was a good balance of spiritual growth, outreach, and leadership training. Everyone was so excited. Well, apparently, not *everyone*.

Tim continued, "Three board members have teenagers, and all three of those kids are graduating next month. They don't come to youth group. I've tried to meet with each of the kids, but they're just not interested."

In my office later that day, it was hard not to think about what happened to Tim. The older teenagers (ages 17 and 18) of three church leaders were making choices (spiritually and otherwise) that brought regret and panic to the parents. These board members assumed a youth pastor would be the savior, bringing their children back to God in a year or less. When this didn't happen, it wasn't important to them that the middle schoolers and younger high schoolers were flocking to youth group and bringing friends.

Unfair? Yes. Unusual? Unfortunately not.

I couldn't help but think of others. Nathan was fired because his senior pastor turned out to be insecure. Nathan's student ministry was growing, and whole families were coming to the church as it became known for meeting the needs of kids. Nathan found out afterward that the pastor had a track record of firing the youth pastor after a year or two—just long enough for a new person to get established and get things happening.

Jessica, in youth ministry just outside of Boston, left her church after three years. The ministry had gone quite well, actually, and the church was surprised and sad when she resigned. But Jessica's soul was sinking. She found the worship style and preaching hard to connect with. She felt lonely in the church, since there were no other young adults in the congregation. Occasionally a parent would get angry and in her face over something ("The group was an hour late getting back from the retreat!" "My kid says you play favorites in the group!") and she found it took her weeks to recover. Kid misbehavior, such as not getting quiet at night on retreats, was becoming increasingly annoying. She just couldn't see herself doing this long term.

> Early on, even in the interview process, set up healthy boundaries about what you can/will be able to do. Be extremely clear on your paradigm and practice of ministry to students, being sure it meshes with the pastor's view.
>
> (BURNED OUT, BAPTIST, SUBURBAN OKLAHOMA)

Maybe you know someone who has been forced out of a youth ministry position. Or maybe it's someone who left a ministry due to exhaustion and personal issues. This book is about helping to keep the "forced out" and "burned out" from happening to you, or to keep it from happening again if it already has. It is about not only avoiding the potholes that can cause you to stumble, but also learning how to soar as a youth worker.

I've done a lot of research, reading, and thinking about these issues. But probably even more important is the fact that I've struggled personally with both burnout and "force out" myself, and you'll see some of this in the chapters that follow.

I've made some spectacular errors as a youth pastor as well. For example, I thought it would be so cool to darken our basement youth room (which was 100' x 40') by not only turning out all the lights but also by putting black plastic over the exit signs. And then I thought it would be so cool to get half the group on one end and half the group on the other (50 kids total), have them get on all fours, and see which team could get to the opposite wall first. What was I thinking? Obviously I wasn't. It was so dark you couldn't see your hand in front of your face. Kids obediently raced toward the opposite wall on their hands and knees. Surprise! (?) Two heads met in the center, and we had to take one kid to the emergency room. Thank God (no kidding!) he wasn't paralyzed, or dead on arrival. Perhaps I'd been watching too many action movies where people jump right up unharmed after explosions or five-story falls. I don't know, but the evening could have resulted in a paralyzed (or worse) son or daughter, a lawsuit, and my dismissal.

## GOOD NEWS ABOUT YOUTH MINISTRY AND YOUTH WORKERS

### Youth Pastor Staying Power

Fortunately, most youth pastors don't get fired or leave their positions overwhelmed by negative factors. In truth, the picture is quite positive. Surprised by this statement? Take the following quiz:

> How long does the typical youth pastor stay in a full-time church youth ministry position?
>
> A) _____18 MONTHS
>
> B) _____ 18 MONTHS
>
> C) _____ ALL OF THE ABOVE
>
> D) _____ NONE OF THE ABOVE

The correct answer is D! The "18 month" figure that often gets cited is a total myth! Whenever I see this figure in print, I contact the author to ask about his/her research base. There is no research base! Someone came up with that number, people began quoting it, and everyone assumes it is true. But there have been several sociologically sound studies of this, and they have shown the figure to be between 3.7 and 4.8 years.[1] The average length of stay in my 2006 survey of 373 fired or burned-out youth pastors was 4.8 years. It would be great, of course, if the average stay were much longer, but the point is that there is nothing foundational or essentially problematic with youth ministry as a calling or career. Men and women leave their positions in church youth ministry after about the same amount of time as senior pastors and other church staff.[2] Their reasons for leaving, both positive and negative, are very similar to the reasons other pastors cite for leaving. [3]

## Youth Ministers Enjoy Significant "Pluses" as They Stay Put

In fact, there are a number of good reasons why a particular youth minister might choose to stay in the same position long term. Surprised? Well, head for your nearest Starbucks, grab a grande mocha (send me the bill...just kidding!), and ponder these practical good things we can experience in long term youth ministry.

1. **Increased Credibility**. Kids aren't stupid. If they've experienced a revolving door of youth leaders who hang around for nine to twelve months and then hit the road, they are going to be reluctant to open up to us. But as the months turn into years, they will see our obvious commitment and our obvious care.

   In my fourth (of fourteen) years at one church, I took the youth group Christmas caroling on "porno row" in downtown Seattle. The kids (and their parents) were a little skeptical, but they listened to my reasons for wanting to do this and agreed. There's no way I could have pulled that off after only six months as youth pastor! (One of my goals was to help our kids, especially those from home school or Christian school situations, experience a little stress, potential embarrassment, or even verbal persecution, so as to strengthen their faith. Mission accomplished! In fact, this experience was so popular that we did it many successive Christmases, bringing light to a very dark place.)

Assuming we're not totally incompetent, our credibility with parents will also increase over time. When I graduated from seminary at age 25 and went to my first church, I thought of myself as an adult, and I expected to be respected as one. No such luck! Many parents viewed me as just an older kid. Credibility began to come, though, as I stayed put. Now, in the church where I've been a volunteer youth worker for over a decade, I'm older—*a lot* older—than the *parents* of the junior highs, and they often express appreciation for my presence.

2. **The Joy of Watching Young People Grow Up.** It really is amazing to watch young people grow. Think of it: At 12 years old they come in skinny, awkward, and shy. What a change we can witness in the next five or six years! God's creative work is astonishing in adolescent development, and it is such a privilege to have a part in the process. These days I often think about Conner and Ricci. I miss them on Wednesday nights because they've graduated up into the senior high group. Along with some of the other boys, they would bring their Razor scooters to youth group. I didn't want to be left out, so I bought one and brought mine as well. Conner and Ricci took great delight in mentoring me on the finer points of scootering. When I see them at church or around town these days, it makes me smile to see how well they're adjusting to the big world of high school.

3. **Lower Stress.** The longer we stay in youth ministry, the more experience we get at handling tough times. Take a few laps around the calendar track, and those youth ministry "biggies"—like retreats, conventions, and major programs—don't seem so overwhelming.

Over time, you'll also learn how to support your kids through the various struggles and challenges they might face in adolescence. When it comes to personal disasters, very little comes as a surprise anymore. I have seen just about everything—leadership team member gets pregnant, a 16-year-old runs off to another state with her Sunday school teacher (whom I recruited) and gets married, my life gets threatened. I've had to advise a 17-year-old who was leading a big program what to do if any of the disgruntled parishioners who had threatened to picket the event tried to storm the stage and grab the microphone. Over the years we learn from our experiences, so that even in the most difficult situations our youth might face (suicide attempts, hate mail, fatal accidents, kids in jail) we are able to be a supportive presence.

Of course, these crises are never fun, but when we experience them, it prepares us for the next time. When you've been in youth ministry for as long as I have, you've seen the dark side of the Christian church and the underside of people's souls. By the amount of human wreckage that washes up at my office door, I recognize we're in a spiritual battle. That high tide of pain can wash us away and out of ministry, or it can, by God's grace, strengthen us to serve him better. The longer we stay in youth ministry, the longer our memory log of badness. Experience serves to make us steadier and stronger when the next tragedy or crisis hits.

> Initially, make a good match of your philosophy and the church's. Continually practice good communication.
>
> (BURNED OUT, NONDENOMINATIONAL, SUBURBAN GERMANY)

4. **Control Over Schedule.** The more experienced we get at planning and massaging the yearly schedule, the easier it gets to do so with our own sanity and our family's needs in mind.

5. **Youth Ministry Keeps Us Young.** This isn't a big concern when we're 22, but past 30 it can become an issue. I'm appalled at how old some of my chronological peers seem. For some folks, getting older means getting close-minded, rigid, and physically (way) out of shape. We can't stay in

youth ministry without being open, flexible, and growing as a person. Being with teenagers helps us keep growing and learning ourselves.

6. **Stay and It May Begin to Pay.** We're not in it for the money, right? Yet it doesn't hurt to receive a wage that helps us put a roof over our head, raise a family, give cheerfully to the Lord's work, and put a little money aside for the future. More and more churches are realizing that long-term youth ministry people are valuable and worth the price to keep. When I left my position as a full-time youth pastor and became a youth ministry professor my own salary went *down* exactly 50 percent. Although I've never done a formal survey, I've talked with many other members of the Association of Youth Ministry Educators, and I've never found a youth ministry educator who did not experience an income reduction when moving from a church-based youth ministry position to a teaching position at a Christian college or seminary.[4]

7. **The Joy of Being Good at Something.** It is fun to do something well, and to sense God's affirmation of our gifts in ministry. If we have a long-term perspective, we learn to capitalize on our strengths and gather around us people who are good where we are not. I'm not a good counselor (Actually, I dread it); musically, I am laughably incompetent; I have no high-profile collegiate or professional sports career in my past. I don't wow 'em as a retreat speaker, either. But I do know how to create a positive atmosphere in a group of kids. I know how to motivate kids to deepen their walks with God. I love to *enfold, encourage, equip, and unleash* youth as well as adults working with youth. I love to organize things and then watch others (including youth) be up front.

It's a good feeling to be good at a few things, and to use the strengths God has given me.

8. **The Joy of Watching Problem People Graduate Out of Our Lives.** No youth worker can relate equally well to everyone or please everyone. I am no exception. Some

youth, over the years, didn't "connect" with me very well. Many of these kids were able to connect better with other adults in the ministry, and I thanked God for it. Some were constantly critical of me personally. Of course, I try to reconcile, hang out, build bridges, etc.—but at some point I cease spending lots of emotional energy in their direction, aside from prayer. Because I know that, sooner or later, the happy day comes...they graduate!

Think of it...when it comes to problem people, a senior pastor has no such graduation day to look forward to. The senior pastor has to wait until problem people either leave or die. It may be a lonngggg wait, too. Youth workers seldom have to wait longer than five years.

9. **Things Get Easier and Take Less Time.** Bible studies, Sunday school lessons, and retreats used to take me hours to get ready for. I spent at least 20 hours preparing personally for my first weekend retreat, and even with that, it was memorable to me only for the spiritual disaster it precipitated. I had prepared three messages from Revelation 3:15-16 ("I know your deeds, that you are neither cold nor hot. I wish you were either one or the other! So, because you are lukewarm—neither hot nor cold—I am about to spit you out of my mouth.")

You can see it, can't you? The first message on "hot," the second on "cold," and the final message, around the campfire on Saturday night, on "lukewarm" with an invitation to go from lukewarm to hot. I noticed afterward that one guy seemed really touched as he walked alone back and forth around the camp for an hour afterward. I thought to myself, "Yes, God is really working on this guy. He's going to be a spiritual giant!" The next morning I asked him if he'd made a decision the night before, but to my surprise he ignored the question. And he *never* came to church or youth group again, much to the chagrin of his parents. It soon became quite apparent he had chosen "cold!"

My 20th weekend retreat didn't take nearly so long to prepare for, and turned out far better. And my 70th weekend retreat took less than three hours of my time in advance (aside from prayer) and was an experience of heaven few will forget.

If we keep doing the programmatic basics of most student ministries—talks, Bible studies, retreats, etc.—these basics become easier, as we get a better feel for what works and what doesn't.

## Youth Ministry is Missional

The nine things listed above are all good and wonderful, but the best news about youth ministry today is that youth workers are connecting to the kingdom of God—what God is doing in the world.

> It pays to have a well-thought-out philosophy/theology of ministry, including how you will help parents. It's so easy, especially for new youth pastors, to be excited about a job and not take care to see if it is really going to be a "good fit."
>
> (BURNED OUT, UNITED METHODIST, URBAN IOWA)

It could be my friend Oluatasu in Nigeria who rents electric generators, borrows computers, and hauls it all to rural villages and runs "Internet Camps" for youth. Or it could be Geomar in the Philippines who runs an "Extreme Camp" on a mountain a couple of hours from Manila. Youth come by the dozens every time he runs one of these camps, which are kind of a combination of *Survivor* and *The Amazing Race*. It could be Alison in County Antrim north of Belfast in Northern Ireland, working with local churches and inspiring them to involve youth in leadership of Sunday services and increase the priority of youth ministry overall. Or it could be Fernando opening a youth center in the Bronx (which, for some of us, may seem like a foreign country unto itself). Some of us might see the kids Fernando works with as "destined for prison," but he views them as peer-influencers— and many are responding to his patient incarnational approach to youth ministry.

A friend of mine often quotes Ephesians 2:10: "For we are God's handiwork, created in Christ Jesus to do good works, which

God prepared in advance for us to do." He daily prays for his ministry with the words, "Lord, what have you prepared in advance for me to do *today*?"

That what we do as youth workers connects directly to the kingdom is good news. It reminds us of the bigger picture when we face obstacles and setbacks.

## Youth Ministry is Intergenerational

Men and women who stay in church-based youth ministry soon realize we are in a partnership with parents in passing on the faith to young people. Though parents may not see us as qualified to give them insights on parenting until we have teenagers ourselves, most of them will see us as youth-culture experts. We can help parents better understand the world their kids are experiencing. We also can help youth understand the concerns of their parents.

Additionally, a youth pastor may be the only adult in a young person's life who really takes that kid seriously. We show kids that adults can care, can be interested, and can value who they are now, not just who they are becoming. Sandra is the youth pastor of a huge African-American church in New York City. Her philosophy of ministry is simple: "God uses youth." She equips and places youth in leadership positions where most of us would place adult volunteers or parents. The 1000-plus youth she works with understand Rev. Sandra not only believes in Jesus but also *believes in them.*

That youth ministry is intergenerational is good news. Youth need to build connections with adults, and there are not that many arenas in our society where this is happening.

## Youth Ministry is Emergent

Recently, my wife and I were in a tiny church in England, a couple of hours southwest of London. It was built in Norman times, and on the back wall is a continuous list of the pastors who have served the church. The list begins in the year *1307*(!). About 40 people were gathered for that morning's worship service. I looked around and realized that my wife and I—both in our 50s—were the youngest people there, *by far*. I'm not sure that congregation will survive even another 10 or 15 years.

Closer to home, my wife and I travel a lot in New England. The summer weather is not as humid as New York City's, and the gentle hills are beautiful. I call New England "the land of closed churches." You see them everywhere—church buildings converted into restaurants, antique stores, pottery or glass-blowing shops, or even private homes. There are plenty of church buildings for sale as well.

It seems the little church in England and the empty churches in New England have at least one thing in common: They have failed or are failing to emerge into the culture that surrounds them. Somehow their expression of Christianity got fossilized... optimal for a certain kind of person with a certain preference for how things could and should be done.

Youth ministry helps the church keep emerging. I fully realize some churches have no interest in changing—and doing youth ministry in such a church can be draining and discouraging. However, many churches change, if only out of pure self-interest, to accommodate the tastes and preferences of each upcoming generation.

A sociologist would explain the process in this way: Most religious parents want their children to be religious as well. This "passing on the faith" impulse implies that parents (feeling inadequate to foster religious transmission on their own) want their kids to be part of, and even like, church. In a religious "free market" (such as in the United States, where there is no official state religion) *churches compete for market share*. Parents who feel a congregation is not "meeting the needs" of their family are likely to switch to a church that is innovating in ways that keep and attract children/ youth/families.

The Seattle church I served for 14 years as youth pastor is a good example. We had a biblically-based mission/vision that oriented us toward wanting to reach the lost. In coming to this mission/vision, we studied the Word, prayed, discussed, and prayed some more. We didn't sit around and say, "Let's increase our market share"—but a sociologist would understand our decision to do "outreach" as a desire to increase "market share." One outcome of this decision was that our youth ministry "farmed" the local zip code. That is, twice annually for three years, we did a mailing to every household in a particular zip code, highlighting opportunities for children and youth as well as special seminars for parents that we held at the local middle school. We knew that the 16,500 households we mailed to would not all have teenagers, but those others might have children who will become teenagers one day or senior citizens concerned about their grandchildren who also live within the reach of the church.

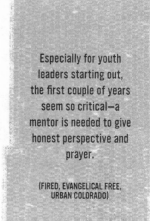

Especially for youth leaders starting out, the first couple of years seem so critical—a mentor is needed to give honest perspective and prayer.

(FIRED, EVANGELICAL FREE, URBAN COLORADO)

To make our church more family-friendly, we built a new addition that included 4000 square feet of nursery and an equivalent-sized youth center. We contoured the morning service to appeal to a variety of musical tastes. We made sure the preaching was both biblical and related to real life.

What happened as a result of these efforts? About a hundred new people from that zip code became part of the church. We had a visible impact on the zip code's middle school, with 50 of our students there. When most of them wore their youth group t-shirts on the same day, you might say our youth ministry was very visible.

That youth ministry is emergent is good news, especially for the church. We may feel unappreciated and undervalued, but we are part of a critically important process in helping the church stay connected to its culture.

## Youth Ministry is Culturally Transformative

The research was first conducted and published in the United Kingdom. Sociologists around the world wondered if what was true in the UK was also true in South Africa, Hong Kong, the U.S., Brazil, and Australia. The data rolled in from every continent, and the results are clear and no longer in dispute. This data caused revolutions in some of the sociology departments at some U.S. universities. Previously, professors had felt free to disparage and ridicule religion. Now those same professors can only quietly reminisce about the good ol' days when it was fashionable to think religion was stupid and didn't make any difference in people's lives.

So what was this information that caused all the fuss worldwide? It was the research from a series of studies showing that Christian youth have *assets* their less religious peers do not have. Some of these "assets" are the absence of something negative for society.[5] In comparison to their irreligious peers, Christian youth are less likely to commit suicide,[6] they are less sexually active,[7] they drink and do drugs less,[8] and they are less likely to break the law and go to jail.[9] Other "assets" mark the presence of something positive for society. Christian youth stay in school longer,[10] are healthier,[11] feel better about themselves,[12] and are more likely to volunteer their time to help others.[13]

Sociologists use the term *religiosity* to refer to expressions of faith such as prayer, Bible reading, attitudes about God, and church or youth group attendance. So here is the key, which helps us as youth workers understand we're doing something important not only for the kingdom but for the wider society: Youth group participation is a part of this "youth religiosity" the academics are measuring. And the good news is that this participation affects what kids believe, and that this makes a positive difference in how they behave.

Of course, we can all think of "Christian" kids who've made horrible choices, but the data shows a strong link between religiosity and assets. The research was so compelling in the U.K. that the researchers said to Parliament, "We need to build more prisons (because most of our young people are headed there eventually) or find a way to support religion among youth."[14] Parliament, ever mindful of finances, felt it would be much cheaper to support religion than to build and staff more prisons. Thus, there was a mandate in the Education Act of 1988 (further strengthened in the Education Act of 1994) that there would be one hour of religious instruction or worship in every school in the UK *every day.*

(This may seem very odd to those of us in the United States, but realize that the UK has an official state religion, The Church of England.)

Many reading this will be familiar with the *National Study of Youth and Religion* conducted by Denton and Smith and published under the title *Soul Searching*.[15] Smith and Denton provide a book-length treatment of the influence of religious beliefs in the lives of young people. (Also interesting is their suggestion that some U.S. denominations are much more successful than others at fostering youth religiosity.)

If you've not been aware of this piece of good news about youth ministry, remember and realize the phenomenon is worldwide. For example, a study of hundreds of late-teenage youth by Fehring (and others) in Australia and South Africa determined that there was an inverse correlation between religiosity and sexual activity (higher religiosity meant less sexual activity).[16] Another study, this time by Nicholas among black South African youth, showed significantly less sexual activity among youth who were religious.[17]

Other studies have found good news related to religious activity and substance abuse. In the United Kingdom, Sutherland and Shepherd looked at a host of substance abuse issues among nearly 500 youth (ages 11 to 16) from five schools. Religiosity was correlated negatively with substance abuse, and the effect was more pronounced among older youth.[18] Similar results were found in Hungary, where outward forms of religiosity were illegal only 11 years ago. A study by Piko and Fitzpatrick of 1240 youth in Szeged, Hungary, found that high religiosity meant lower substance abuse.[19]

That youth ministry impacts our culture and society is good news. It is so easy to feel that we youth workers are wasting our time, or that we'd be better off doing something "more important." Well-meaning pastors and other adults in our churches may even try to counsel us to get a "real job" or do something that "has a future." But in youth ministry, we're actually creating a future—and a good one at that.

# CHAPTER 2
# EARLY HAZARDS

## THE VALLEY OF THE SHADOW: THE "MORALE CURVE TROUGH"

From the world of business comes a slice of truth we experience whenever we start a new ministry. It could be our first ministry, or it could be our zillionth. Virtually everyone who goes to a new job will cycle through a predictable range of the feelings. There is often a period of low morale that tends to hit between four and six months after arriving at a new job.[1] Too often, people bail out during this period at the bottom, or trough, of the morale curve, never realizing these "lows" are a natural part of the cycle.

FIGURE 1: MORALE TROUGH CURVE

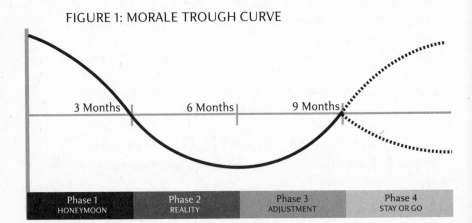

| Phase 1 HONEYMOON | Phase 2 REALITY | Phase 3 ADJUSTMENT | Phase 4 STAY OR GO |

Most people go through four phases after taking a new job position.

*Phase 1: The Honeymoon.* We land in a new ministry position with much enthusiasm and optimism. Kids are happy to see us; parents are grateful we've come. We feel good about our new church and its senior pastor. Everything, or at least nearly everything, looks great. It's why we've come. We're ready to roll. Our adrenaline is pumping as we launch.

*Phase 2: Reality Sets In.* "You mean the youth group has always staffed children's church—and that means I'm in charge of that, too? Why didn't anyone bother to tell me this before?"

"Gosh, I'm realizing how much I miss my parents and my brother back home, 300 miles away now."

"You mean my office is in the basement next to the water heater?"

"I'm going to be out six nights a week, *every* week."

> The presence of a mentor in the first two years of ministry can help a youth minister understand how to balance ministry, family, and personal life.
>
> (BURNED OUT, ROMAN CATHOLIC, RURAL INDIANA)

No matter how wonderful our new ministry position, some aspects of the place and the job will not be exactly as we envisioned. If we had close ties with our previous church, we will feel the loss deeply. We miss the people and places we called home. Like peeling back layers of wallpaper in an old fixer home, the challenges may seem overwhelming as we learn more and more of what the new job really entails and what's expected of us. For many, the worst feelings of discouragement come four to six months after arriving.

This was especially true for me when I left my longtime position at a Seattle church and headed to a new ministry position in New Jersey. The church in New Jersey was fine, but after a few months I was in mourning. I missed the Seattle people, of course, but I missed much more than that. Somehow in the candidating process at the new church I didn't ask about where my office would be. Behold...it turned out to be a tiny cement-block-walled rectangle with an old metal desk, a rickety chair, and a single small window looking out on the church garbage dumpster. It was kind of a step down from the Seattle situation where I'd had a beautiful, second-floor, lakeview office in the old English mansion our church owned, with leaded glass windows on three sides, plus a bay window to sit in when I wanted to think, read, or pray. Now you might think that if I'd been more spiritual this jarring change wouldn't have mattered. Well, it did matter, and I struggled for a while with what I'd given up to come to the New Jersey church.

*Phase 3: Adjustment Attempts.* Some youth workers resign after just a few months. The weight of reality is more than they can shoulder; it's time to feel a calling to a different situation. Most of us, however, carry on. At least we do for a while.

Once we understand the realities of our particular situation (our pastor is not very supportive, the parents tend to gripe, we can't afford to live in a nice apartment, and children's chapels plus daily Vacation Bible School is unalterably on our job description), we try to adjust. One by one we come to terms with the negatives. Can we live with them? Can we change them? Are we capable of doing this? We take the realities of the situation and compare them with the resources we have. We put all these ingredients into our mental stew and stir. Then we decide if the result is palatable.

In both my Seattle and New Jersey churches, I inherited a strong tradition of an annual graduation banquet. I have nothing against food and fellowship, but banquets have always seemed a bit of a minefield to me. People tend not to sign up or buy tickets on time, which causes food planning or caterer contracting to be difficult. Then there are the issues of the program, the decorations, the cleanup, and often the "after banquet" activities. Whew! Makes me weary just thinking about it.

In the Seattle church we eventually replaced the banquet with taking the seniors, at church expense, to a "Grad Overnight" retreat at a beautiful resort center. Noting that seniors were not generally the committed leaders of the group (as I'd hoped), but instead tended to drop out altogether, complaining that they missed their older friends or that the group seemed immature with "all those freshmen," I not only changed the grad event from a banquet to a retreat, but had the event in October instead of May/June. Why? The retreat setting gave me the chance to gently address the drop-out issue while there was still time to make a difference.

In one of the sessions I discovered a certain flow that, happily, resulted in many of the seniors seriously committing to continued attendance, involvement, and leadership. Here are the steps I followed:

1) We began by just sitting around and reminiscing about great youth group memories of the past. We laughed so hard we sometimes cried remembering all the fun and funny things that had become part of our "holy history."

2) I then asked them to remember the seniors they'd looked up to and enjoyed so much back when they were freshmen. This became another joyful and sometimes poignant trip down memory lane. I usually interjected the question, "How glad are you they were involved in the group?"

3) "Can anyone think why I bring this all up now? It's because *you* are, right now, the ones whom the freshmen look up to. *You* are the ones they admire. And believe me, when you were freshmen, those seniors who added so much to your time in the group all had complaints about your immaturity and how they missed their older friends." For many present at the grad retreat, year after year, this was a moment of epiphany. I acknowledged that the ministry is not targeted primarily at them, but at the younger students. I affirmed their great maturity and told them this was their chance to be leaders and to *be there* for the younger ones who looked up to them as gods.

In the New Jersey church "Thou shalt not mess with the annual grad banquet" was like the 11th Commandment, so there wasn't the freedom to replace it with a retreat. But at least I was able to give it a fun twist. I got the (crazy) idea that Donald Trump would give us exclusive use of the eight-stories-high atrium and café in his half-billion-dollar headquarters building in New York City. If you've seen *The Apprentice* you've seen inside views of Trump

Tower. I thought we could charter a bus, head into the city, and have an exquisite dessert in a setting that was a quantum leap nicer than the church fellowship hall. I put on my best suit and took the train into the city.

The Trump corporate headquarters are on the 23rd floor of the Trump Tower on 5th Avenue. I introduced myself and my purpose to the receptionist with these words: "Hello, my name is Rev. Leonard Kageler and I'm the youth pastor of Long Hill Chapel in New Jersey. We're holding a formal high school graduation banquet at our church this coming June 5th. I'd like to bring the 50 students on a chartered bus here at 10:30 p.m. and have exclusive use of the atrium for our dessert. I would like free and exclusive use of the facility for two hours—though, of course, we would pay for the dessert."

Get a good mentor, someone who understands both you and the ministry.

(BURNED OUT, ASSEMBLIES OF GOD, URBAN MALAYSIA)

Have you ever been driving at night and come across a deer, and watched its round eyes widen in your headlights? That was the look the receptionist gave me. She hesitated and said, "Could you say that all again?" I repeated myself and handed her the proposal in written form in a very fancy folder. "I'll have to check about this," she replied.

She disappeared for a moment to give it to someone else. I sat there (praying) for about 15 minutes, picturing my proposal being sent up the chain of command, and then coming back down. Eventually, a businessman (not Trump) emerged from a side door with my proposal in hand. With a smile he extended his hand to me. "Rev. Kageler? Yes, we think this will be fine. How can we further serve you?"

It's nice when our attempts to adjust negative things in our job description actually work out well.

*Phase Four: Stay and Grow, or Exit.* This decision point comes about nine to twelve months into a new job. Do we stay and try to work things out, or do we head for the copy shop to print an updated resume? Even if we survive the "morale curve trough," we may get to Phase Four and conclude it's just not worth the hassle to stay.

We experience the morale curve not only when we move to a new job, but also when our job description changes.

Though we cannot do much to prevent the morale curve, there are steps we can take that affect how high the highs are and how low the lows are. The highs and lows depend somewhat on how much accurate information we have about our jobs before we get there. The clearer our picture of what we'll face in advance, the more we'll understand the negatives when we arrive. If our honeymoon in Phase One is not so high, we won't have as far to fall in Phase Two. The more realistic our appraisal of our situation, the easier it is to adjust (Phase Three) and move ahead (Phase Four), because we've foreseen these problems.

It's also comforting just to realize that this progression of feelings and experiences is absolutely normal. Getting into Phase Four and choosing to stay can result in increasing effectiveness as we do the work of ministry.

## IDEALISM: BAMBI VS. GODZILLA

Another early danger relates to our own idealism. We come into youth ministry fresh, innocent, idealistic, and so sincere. We romp through the morale curve trough undaunted and proceed toward the high meadows. We believe this is the way it will always be. We may be too starry-eyed and distracted to hear the thudding footsteps of some monster issue or crisis approaching. Then... splat. We are crushed by the facts and realities in our own youth ministry. This collision of reality and idealism sends some youth workers packing—choosing to find a better place or a better line of work.

What are some of these "Godzillas of reality"?

**1. How Christian People Should Act.** We work in the church, right? It's full of Christians, right? People who believe in grace and forgiveness and want to live out the fruit of the Spirit, right? Don't count on it.

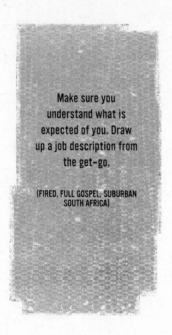

Make sure you understand what is expected of you. Draw up a job description from the get-go.

(FIRED, FULL GOSPEL, SUBURBAN SOUTH AFRICA)

"Len, you've been here five months, and I'm convinced your true purpose is to destroy this youth group and all that Matt tried to build." These words were said to me in my first church after seminary. They were said loudly, with anger, and in front of ten young people, in the middle of what was supposed to be a nice social. Guess what? I didn't sleep very well that night.

Or how about this one? "Len, in this notebook we've written down all the mistakes we feel you've made in the last several years. If we don't get what we want from you tonight, we will make what's here public." A marriage in the youth staff had blown apart. Another staffer was charged with causing the breakup. Everyone had chosen sides. Some had decided it was all my fault.

Sometimes it's not the congregation, but the senior pastor. Consider these words from one of the youth pastors in our survey: "Father treated people very cruelly, referring to one staff person as a 'fat cow.' He drove out several youth pastors over the years in our parish."

We have it in our minds that Christians should act like Christians in the church. The reality is that sometimes they don't, and woe be it to us if we get in harm's way. When things don't go the way they've hoped, some people feel they need someone to blame, someone to kick, someone to destroy. More than once, I have been the unfortunate recipient of a crusade of terror—and it's been like a nightmare.

**2. What Youth Ministry Should Be Like.** We might envision that youth ministry will be a glorious series of revivals, in which we spend all our time leading kids to Christ, counseling them, and guiding them spiritually. Any church-based youth pastor who's been around awhile will affirm that youth ministry, properly done, involves an immense amount of deskwork and administration. But youth workers are not famous for their love of administration.

From our youth ministry desk, we might expect that the people of our church will be eager to see changes that will help accomplish the mission of reaching and discipling people for Christ. Are you in a church like that? If so, praise God! Some of the rest of us must subsist on crumbs of progress rationed out sparingly by church boards and committees.

We also have the idea that things should be fair within the church. We expect that our senior pastors and church boards will deal fairly with problems and issues. Unfortunately, that's not always the case. Thank God if you've never seen unfairness in the church!

**3. Our Own Authority.** We're called to lead, innovate, and inspire, right? As a youth pastor, each of us expects to be respected as a leader. That Bambi-type idealism is easily crushed. If we're under 30, and especially if we don't have any kids of our own, many adults will give us respect that is only slightly above what they give to a 14-year-old. Our decisions can be undermined, our motives questioned.

**4. The Youth Themselves.** We expect kids to be hungry for God as we teach and lead them. We expect they'll like our ideas and have a deep commitment to the Lord and the youth group.

Although some kids are radically committed to Christ, the sad fact is that many are not. Greg doesn't come to Bible studies so he can grow deep in the Word of God; he comes so he can sit by Ellen. Marlene doesn't come to the Friday night social happy about reaching out to new kids and helping shy ones feel included; she's excited because her parents are away for the weekend and two of her friends from the group are coming over to spend the night after the event. She's *very* excited because she's rented three R-rated movies. Not violent movies, of course ("Why do boys like that stuff, anyway?"). There will be lots of romance, though, lots of skin, and lots of sex. Marlene's still a virgin, but that's a stigma she hopes to shed soon.

It can be a real blow when we realize just how totally seduced by the world many of our kids are. We may find it very hard to love kids who live way below what we expect of them. But if we don't love our kids, we'll quickly find an excuse to leave.

We may also believe that, as the months and years go by, more and more youth will join the youth group because of our wonderful ministry. I sure felt this way. I got a heavy dose of reality when statistics showed that youth group growth *and* decline seemed to have far more to do with the Sunday morning worship attendance of our church than whatever changes I made in the youth ministry itself.

## CHANGING HEARTS, CHANGING BODIES

Many of us are quite young when we first begin working in the field of youth ministry. We may start out strong, with energy that rivals that of our young people. But then our passion for youth may fade. Our own maturation can mean work with youth becomes more and more of a cross-cultural ministry. As we age, this internal rewiring of passion and preferences means many leave youth ministry for the pulpit or other kinds of ministries.

Physically, it's easy to go downhill in a hurry past 30. If there's always something better to do than to get regular exercise, and if there's always another day to start eating right, we won't get far into our 30s before our bodies resemble the contours of apples or pears. It's a rare apple or pear that can maintain the energy level that good youth ministry requires.

Try this mental exercise. Close your eyes, and picture yourself with 30 extra pounds on your body. Open your eyes and know this: *This is your future*—unless you make a decision to make it untrue. And know this: If you don't decide to work actively toward a healthy lifestyle, you've decided to have a life that will increasingly be hindered, complicated, and ultimately shortened because of the medical consequences of being overweight.

The average American gains 1.5 pounds each year of his or her entire adult life.[2] That is 30 pounds in 20 years. Don't believe me? Go to the mall of your choice, have a seat, and watch people. Try to picture what these people looked like when they were twenty. How much heavier are they now, do you think?

Please understand: I'm not being sucked in by the world's obsession with a beautiful body and thinness. I'm pleading for your ability to continue effectively in youth ministry—or any ministry for that matter—in the future. At the very least, that extra 30 pounds is going to slow you down, and one by one you'll have to kiss good-bye things you used to be able to do and enjoy.

I made the decision to stay fit while in seminary. My wife made the same decision, and we support each other in this commitment. We agreed to never buy larger clothes from that day forward (except for pregnancy, of course!). Today, over 30 years later, we're both still wearing those same size jeans.

Staying in shape requires a "no" and a "yes". The "no" has to do with food intake. I'm careful what I eat during the workweek, and I pretty much eat what I want (within reason) on the weekends. Believe me, I know the calorie count of most drinks at Starbucks (doing the grande mocha with skim milk and no whip knocks it down from around a horrendous 600 calories to a bad 400). I used to think muffins were kinda healthy, until I learned that the ones at my favorite bakery are 600 to 800 calories each (nearly half the calories you'd normally burn in a day).

> Network at the local level. Make sure you have at least one day off weekly, and that you're not out more than four nights a week for youth ministry.
>
> (BURNED OUT, NONDENOMINATIONAL, URBAN IRELAND)

Recently I attended a college basketball game in Madison Square Garden. Each member of the family sitting in front of us (mom, dad, two kids, all overweight) drank a super-sized soft drink. Did they know the drink alone was about 1000 calories? They also had the large fries, a large hot dog, and...well, you get the point.

The "yes" of staying in shape involves putting regular exercise on the calendar. Some, like myself, are solo exercisers. I wouldn't do it if I had to do it with others. Others won't do it unless it's with other people...on a team, in a fitness class like kick-boxing, or some other setting where there is at least one other person. No matter the key is to do it. My own lifetime fitness goal is to be half-marathon capable. That is, I want to be fit enough to run 13.125 miles on any given day of the week, in any given month, in any given year. To achieve that goal I run three times a week: ten miles on Mondays, seven on Wednesdays, and three (with Oliver, our beagle) each weekend. That may sound extreme to you, but that running time is a great time for prayer and for working out the stress in my life. And, every now and then, I run an official half-marathon and enjoy race-day excitement and ambiance.

## FEELING SAD

It was a cool, rainy Saturday morning in mid-November. I was looking forward to my monthly breakfast with my junior high leaders. I think youth of this age are much more capable of spiritual growth and leadership than people give them credit for, and this group of spiritually motivated and ministry-minded kids was a good case in point.

After we made breakfast together in the church kitchen, it was time to settle down. On the agenda was the happy business of prayer and planning the group activities. September and October had gone very well, and great events were on the calendar for us to look forward to. In the two years I'd been at the church, the junior high ministry had become famous for the right reasons.

"So, before we start planning, how do you feel it's going in the group these days?" I asked.

Jana began. "I think it's going terrible. Sheila, that new girl, is so obnoxious."

"Yeah, I agree," answered Charlie. "None of the events are any fun anymore."

"I don't even look forward to coming," added Karen.

"I don't like it either, and I think my family might start looking for a different church," Ricci added helpfully.

Believe it or not, the conversation went downhill from there. Negativity was expressed with vehemence and bitter conviction. For me, it was an agonizing hour. When they seemed to be done, I asked, "Does anyone have anything positive—anything good about the group—they want to say?"

Seven pairs of eyes looked back at me. No one responded, not even one. I was so totally blown away that all I could do was close with a brief prayer. After spending the next hour taking all of them home in the church van, I went back to my office and sat at my desk, lost in thought. Damage control time. If this had been my first ministry, no doubt I would have composed a resignation letter. I decided instead to do nothing unusual. Why?

"Len, you stupid jerk," I kindly said to myself, "you forgot it is November."

Here's another example. From time to time I get invited to observe another youth ministry, with the idea that I can provide some kind of assessment of what's going on. Recently, I sat in on a youth group session that started out bad and just kept getting worse. Jennifer began by asking the 25 youth present to "Feel free now to share with us all what God is doing in your life or what you are learning from him these days." Blank stares and silence. "Well, let's sing, then," and she launched into a song a capella, which became a solo. Eventually, the youth warmed up a little bit, but not much. Later that day I met with Jennifer. She was so discouraged and devastated—she was even questioning her own call and fitness for ministry, faced with such a spectacular failure.

"Have you ever heard of Seasonal Affective Disorder?" I asked her.

"Yes, of course—but that doesn't *really* affect people, does it?"

Long pause. "Knowing it's November, here are some ideas that may have helped..." It was epiphany time for Jennifer as she realized that even if only a handful of kids are "down," their influence can drag down an entire evening.

November...it's caused more than a few youth workers to get burned out and quit.

Seasonal Affective Disorder (SAD) is a fancy clinical name. In my first few years of ministry, I'd never heard the term, but I did notice that some of my brightest and best youth often went into a spiritual tailspin in November. They'd get negative and critical. They wouldn't feel like talking, sharing, or singing. And I noticed that it wasn't just the young people who seemed affected; so were some adults.

I used to lie awake at night thinking about this...worrying, praying, wondering why. I tried to use counseling or "heavy" talks with the group or individuals as early weapons. It only took a few years to figure out that no amount of prayer, counseling, or extra meetings would make any difference. All I had to do was wait. By mid-or late December, the grumpy kids and adults would snap out of it and be their cheerful and positive selves again.

Seasonal Affective Disorder is very well documented. It's been discussed in the *Journal of the American Medical Association* and *Scientific American*, as well as in popular press like *USA Today*, *Sports Illustrated*, *Business Horizons*, and even *Vogue* (among many others).[3]

SAD exists because of the shortening daylight hours as winter approaches and the change to and from daylight savings time each year. This causes a fluctuation in the amount of daily light we see and is also coupled with changing weather. This change of light level affects the body's production of a chemical called *melatonin*. In some people this change in melatonin level produces symptoms of depression. In other words, people get grumpy. Six weeks is about what it takes to readjust, though some people have the symptoms throughout the winter months.

Youth workers who don't know about this are doubly vulnerable. First, we're vulnerable because we're clueless as to why we might get blindsided by people we thought were on our side. People we've always known as nice, friendly, and supportive suddenly seem to want our ministries filleted and set out as a feast for the circling vultures they and others have become.

Second, we are vulnerable because we may experience SAD ourselves. Things might be going okay and then, without apparent cause or warning, our internal "self-talk" gets negative. We internally rehearse long, critical speeches to kids, board members, or our senior pastor. We compose our resignation letters, dream of how nice it would be to change churches, and speculate about how unjust it is that someone as wonderful as we could be stuck with such ungrateful people.

If you've lived in Florida or Southern California all your life, chances are that you may have never seen SAD. One study showed that the farther north a person went in North America, the greater the percentage of people who were *severely* affected.[4]

Maintain outside relationships and rely on them for balance.

(BURNED OUT, NONDENOMINATIONAL, URBAN NEW YORK)

| FLORIDA | 1.4 PERCENT |
| MARYLAND | 6.3 PERCENT |
| NEW YORK | 8.0 PERCENT |
| NEW HAMPSHIRE | 10.0 PERCENT |

These percentages represent only the most severe cases. An equal percentage of people will experience only moderate symptoms.

What does it mean? If you live in Baltimore, St. Louis, Denver, or Eureka, and you minister to 50 junior and senior high school kids, it's likely that seven or eight will experience the significant emotional undertow of SAD. It's only a small number, but the destructive potential is frightening.

Knowing this, what do I do about SAD?

1. Every November I remind the youth group and volunteer staff about SAD. I tell them that the feelings, if they come, are normal. I implore them not to drop out during this time, but to stay around people who can encourage them.

2. Personally, I have a policy to never, ever resign from *anything* in November.

3. When I go to youth pastor meetings, I try to watch for those who are feeling low and seek ways to encourage them, if I can.

## ANY SOLUTIONS?

In this chapter, we have toured some of the hazards youth workers encounter that cause some of them to choose to get off the bus. Are there any easy solutions to these issues? Actually, there are!

**1. Being Aware.** It sounds almost too simple, but just knowing about hazards like SAD or the morale curve trough will help. Were you unaware? Now, you know about them.

Jim moved from San Diego to Portland, Oregon, when he came to work at his new church. He'd read about SAD and he knew there were a lot of niceties about life in San Diego he would miss dearly. He began his ministry in July and, sure enough, in mid-November, he was feeling the pull toward home. He put a big picture of the ocean up in his office, and he shared his feelings openly with the pastoral staff and other youth pastors he saw frequently. He made it through his first winter and now, three years later, he's an avid backpacker. He loves Portland and how close the mountains are. The ocean picture in his office has been replaced by a photo of Mt. Hood.

**2. Being Real.** Having our ideals crushed by reality is never fun. Youth workers who survive the shattering of early ideals do so largely because they truly love young people, they deeply feel a call from God to be in youth ministry, and they have a support network.

Samantha went to her second church assuming her senior pastor would be warm, supportive, and caring—like her first senior pastor. Surprise! Her new pastor was aloof and never talked at a feeling level; soon Samantha felt she'd made a big mistake. She almost resigned the day after he told her, "Look, I don't need or want to be your friend—get that through your head." Samantha got active with a support group for youth pastors that met monthly. She found several other youth ministers had pastors like that. She successfully let go of her expectations about her pastor, and this group began to meet her needs for caring support.

**3. Being Honest.** There is nothing wrong with changing our minds. You may have set out with high hopes of long-term ministry with kids, but now your heart is calling you in a different direction. It's okay. In fact, it's better to leave than to stay for the wrong reasons.

**4. Being Centered.** The surest way to survive discouragement and setback in the early years of ministry is to remain centered on Jesus Christ. He is our comfort when we hurt, our security when our surroundings shake. The apostle Paul certainly had his share of bad days and setbacks. Listen to his words:

> We are hard pressed on every side, but
> not crushed; perplexed, but not in despair;
> persecuted, but not abandoned; struck down, but
> not destroyed…Therefore, we do not lose heart.
> Though outwardly we are wasting away, yet
> inwardly we are being renewed day by day. For our
> light and momentary troubles are achieving for us
> an eternal glory that far outweighs them all.
>
> 2 CORINTHIANS 4:8-9,16-17

Yes, sometimes it seems like we must slog through the slime to be youth pastors. Yet when we are properly centered on our relationship with Christ, we can keep from being swallowed up.

Some youth workers who start strong eventually decide for themselves that they will change churches or change careers. Unfortunately, others have this decision made for them. They get fired. Some may see it coming. Others are surprised. In either case, it's no fun...

# CHAPTER 3
# CAUTION: CONFLICT AND COMPROMISE

I held the envelope in my hand for a few moments before tearing it open. Seeing the return address, I knew the nature of what was inside.

> Dear Pastor Kageler,
>
> With regards to your so-called youth rally next month, I am writing to inform you again that I feel what you have planned is a godless abomination. I am writing our headquarters and our Christian college presidents, as well as the other pastors in our district to ask them to join me in fasting and prayer, and to call upon God to stop this evil. You will be held accountable by Almighty God for the deception and worldliness you are fostering among our precious young people.
>
> I intend to do everything in my power to stop this event...

**Conflict** \kon'flikt\ 1. to come into collision; 2. to contend; do battle. 3. a battle or struggle, esp. a prolonged struggle.

*Collision...battle...struggle*—these are the words the diction-
ary uses to define conflict. What are the feelings that define it?
Try these: shock, betrayal, confusion, hopelessness, doubt, anger,
and uncertainty. Nearly 100 percent of youth pastors who get fired
name some kind of conflict as the reason. If we think we can be
in youth ministry and avoid conflict, we are fooling ourselves.
Conflict may not result in our getting fired, but it can sure hasten
burnout if we don't come to terms with the issue, particularly in
our first few years of ministry. It's a major ministry hazard.

In my case, the youth rally that so concerned my letter-writer
went ahead as planned with the unanimous support of our church
elders. It was clear to many who attended that the Lord was pow-
erfully present that night. With so much prayer from all over the
country, how could it have been otherwise?

In my survey of youth ministers who were fired or left because
of burnout, respondents could list up to three reasons for their
departure. Those who were fired from a position in youth ministry cited conflict with the following people as primary reasons for
their dismissal:

1. SENIOR PASTOR            49 PERCENT

2. OTHER CHURCH LEADERSHIP  46 PERCENT

3. PARENTS                  15 PERCENT

4. KIDS                     4 PERCENT

If we want to last in youth ministry, we must learn to work
successfully with the four groups of people here. In chapters 7
through 9 we will consider how we can build positive relationships
with each of these groups. But first, let's just try to understand
what the issues are. We'll start with the single biggest source of
youth pastor stomach upset: the senior pastor.

# THE SENIOR PASTOR: FRIEND OR FOE?

A supportive senior pastor can be one of the greatest assets any youth minister can have. If your senior pastor is a regular source of encouragement to you and an advocate for your work with youth, count your blessings.

Unfortunately, not all of us minister in situations like that. There are at least four primary areas of potential conflict between the youth pastor and the senior pastor. Let's consider each of them by listening to some of the responses to my survey of "fired" or "burned-out" youth pastors.

> I learned that if a church brings someone into a job, that person should be trusted and allowed to do the job they were hired to do. I followed a youth pastor who'd been there a long time, and I inherited his leadership team. They wouldn't let me lead or make decisions. I wish I'd understood enough to see the "brick wall" situation I was getting myself into.
>
> (FIRED, BRETHREN, SUBURBAN UNITED KINGDOM)

## 1. Differing Philosophies of Ministry

Two weeks after arriving at a new youth worker job, the founding senior pastor, who had raised the congregation to be one of the largest in the denomination, died of a heart attack. Several months later, I sat in the study of my new senior pastor to discuss my dreams for the youth ministry. I was obviously enthusiastic about building a team that could generate deep and lasting relationships with the church's teenagers. In fact, I was in the process of building such relationships, I continued, and the youth seemed to be responding...

At this point the pastor straightened up in his chair, looked at me across his acre of desk, and said, "If you're going to succeed in a church this size, you can't expect to get too close to the

students. You'll have to keep your distance. This
isn't a small operation, you know."

...In a very short time it became clear to me that
my approach to ministry was out of sync with his.

This conflict didn't result in termination. The youth pastor hung on for a couple of years and then found another position. But it's a perfect example of a philosophy of ministry conflict. The pastor wanted a more managerial approach to ministry, while the youth worker believed in a more relational style. It's very easy to get fired over a difference in ministry philosophies. My survey revealed many such cases.

One frequently cited difference in ministry philosophies concerns the church's attitude toward unchurched kids. Again and again in my survey the issue of church discomfort with non-churched kids came up:

I was fired because my heart and soul were
dedicated to winning unchurched kids to Christ.
He wanted my emphasis to be 99 percent on kids
who were already churched.

A few months into my ministry there I had planned
an outreach event in which our own youth could
bring their non-Christian friends. The pastor,
when he found out about it, told me, "Our youth
group is for our kids only, not their friends. You
are not to try to bring unchurched kids into this
group; the parents don't want it." I resigned on
the spot.

## 2. Pastoral Insecurity

Woe be the youth pastor who has a boss with a poor self-image. Success in the youth ministry, especially if it includes numerical growth, can cause a senior pastor to get uneasy. The congregation might see the youth pastor as a much better communicator than the senior pastor. Here are several such stories from my file of firings:

> Guard yourself and pray. There are people who feel threatened, are jealous, and just plain don't know how to handle REAL or a ministry based on relationships.
>
> (FIRED, NAZARENE, SUBURBAN MISSOURI)

The youth pastor was very intelligent and articulate. He was also warm and very committed to God and to being true before him. He was an excellent leader. So when he saw the church was dying fast, he was concerned and shared some ideas with the senior pastor. The pastor took this as rejection and criticism. He had the church leadership fire the youth pastor.

The pastor was insanely jealous of my success.

She was fired because a very jealous nun dominated our senior pastor and forced him to divert funds away from youth ministry so we could no longer afford the youth pastor's salary. This nun was extremely jealous of the youth pastor's success and resented the new people coming. In her [the nun's] mind the Church exists for Sunday worship, nothing else.

## 3. Scapegoat

It makes us mad. It's not fair. We may even wonder if God exists after seeing it happen—or having it happen to us. I am not, by nature, an angry person, but scapegoat firings really tick me off.

> I had been the youth pastor for ten years. The church had grown in the past and had continued to grow under our new senior pastor. A few of the parents and people of the church were unhappy because we listened to contemporary Christian music in the youth group. These people put a lot of pressure on him. He chose to fire me instead of support me. He thought it would be easier to get a new youth pastor than to get these people to shut up. I was devastated. Well, at least they gave me six months' severance pay.

Does that make you angry? Good.

## 4. New Pastor = New Staff

When a senior pastor resigns, some churches require that the whole pastoral staff must resign, too. This gives the new pastor the opportunity to bring in his or her own team. In churches that don't automatically take this approach, a new senior pastor might still maneuver to get the "old" youth pastor removed.

> Our new pastor told me that the church could no longer afford to pay my salary and that, therefore, I was terminated. I could take my time finding a new position, but it only took me a couple of months. I was glad to get out of there. Four weeks later they hired a new youth pastor at the same salary I was receiving. The new youth pastor was

the son of my new pastor's best friend. Needless to say, it makes me cynical about the politics and power plays that take place in the church.

## CHURCH LEADERSHIP: WHEN IN DOUBT, BLAME IT ON THE YOUTH PASTOR

If we find ourselves in a church that has supportive, visionary, and positive lay leadership, we should drop to our knees daily and thank God. Churches with leadership like that do exist. Unfortunately, we can't just assume that everyone who is in a position of church leadership is gifted with great spiritual wisdom, vision, and insight. When we head into a new church situation, we can't take it for granted that the church board and other church leadership will be a source of blessing and support to us.

> Have a peer accountability structure. Make sure your job description is realistic and that the entire congregation understands it.
>
> (FIRED, ANGLICAN, SUBURBAN AUSTRALIA)

A youth minister's conflicts with other church leadership will often mirror his or her conflicts with the senior pastor. It is not hard for the senior pastor to rally other church leaders in support. In addition, problems with church leadership committees often involve issues of property, finances, and programs. Here are a few comments I've heard (or heard about) over the years:

"The young people have no respect for the church bus. When they're done, it looks like a pig pen."

"They had no right to paint the youth room without consulting the deacons first!"

"Patsy, do you realize that after your program last night the janitor found cigarette ashes in the main bathroom?"

"I don't like the dancing the youth choir does when they sing."

"Why are you having a pudding fight when there are millions of people starving in Africa?"

"There's not enough Bible teaching in Sunday school. When I was that age, we had a 60-minute Bible study every Sunday, and we really learned something."

Remember my Trump Tower Graduation Dessert success story? Only seven months earlier I had a very public and very humiliating disaster that made some board members at that same church doubt not only my judgment, but also my fitness for ministry and, indeed, my sanity! I lost over $6,000 in one hour.

Even before I arrived at the New Jersey church I had begun to plan a large-scale outreach event to take place in October. I'd made arrangements for a very well-known Christian rock singer to come with her band and dance team for an outreach concert. The contract was confidently signed.

Between contract signing and the October concert, many things went wrong. The slick promo posters they'd promised didn't arrive until one week before the concert. I was shocked by the specificity and complexity of their lighting and sound system requirements. It took me a very long time to find a provider that could accomplish their list. The band manager, without my knowledge or consent, fired my provider two weeks before the concert and hired his own. I learned from my own kids and area youth pastors that contemporary Christian music was kind of a foreign concept in New Jersey, very different from the Pacific Northwest.

The day of the concert was a nightmare. The sound/light people arrived at 4 p.m. instead of 9 a.m. We quickly discovered the middle school auditorium did not have enough electrical power for their systems. So at 4:30 I was desperately tracking down the school district's head electrician. The good news was that he could lay a special cable from a main junction box in another building. The bad news was this would cost $100 per hour and might take several hours. The singer and nine-member band flew in from Nashville and were taken to their hotel. Two of my youth group kids accompanied the vans that went to pick them up. These two kids came to the auditorium as we were (frantically) setting up and reported, "She's a witch. What a stuck-up snob!"

The concert itself was worse yet. The band arrived on time, but the sound/light people weren't ready. I took a quick look at the small entourage that arrived with the singer, and asked their road manager, "Where are the dancers your promo stuff bragged about?"

"Oh, that was last year's show. We don't have them anymore."

The sound check *started* at 8 p.m.—the time the concert was supposed to begin. We had 500 people standing outside for over an hour. Thank God it wasn't raining. I was thankful, too, that I'd thought to hire police to stand around. They had a calming effect.

The concert finally started at 9 p.m. With an audience of 500, we were 250 short of our original financial break-even point of 750 attendees. I had hoped and prayed for 1000. I tried to console myself with the words, "So what if I lose my entire youth budget tonight? It will be worth it as kids come to Christ."

About 45 minutes into the concert Ms. Rock Star began giving her "talk" and then her "invitation." I assumed this was the halfway point of the concert. The only kids who "came forward" were my student leaders who were ready to counsel others. Not a single person made any response to the gospel presentation. Ms. Rock Star sang a final song and it was over and done at 10 p.m.—one hour total from start to finish.

You'll find it easy to believe I didn't sleep very well that night. You'll also find it easy to believe the church treasurer was, to put it mildly, really upset!

## PARENTS: THEY LOVE ME, THEY LOVE ME NOT

Parents have a vested interest in youth ministry. They care a great deal about what we are doing, because they entrust their daughters and sons to us each week. A group of actively involved and supportive parents can be a great blessing to any youth ministry.

But if we fail to grasp the parents' point of view very early in our ministry, we guarantee conflict at best and dismissal at worst.

One in six youth pastors who get the ax name conflict with parents as a primary cause. Over what kinds of issues do youth pastors and parents often collide?

## 1. Rules, Standards, and Control

When we enter youth ministry, our first priority is building good rapport with the kids. We want to be seen as nice people. We want to be liked. Junior and senior highers aren't stupid...they know we want them to like us. In fact, *they know our job depends on them.* This can give them a sense of power over us. They know we'll be more lenient with them than their parents are, and some will get maximum mileage out of this situation.

Retreats, lock-ins, and other overnighters—these are all essential items on the youth ministry program menu. We hold these events because they offer the greatest opportunities for ministry. They also offer great opportunities for disaster.

Junior high school kids love to stay up all night. When an all-nighter or a retreat is over, we say good-bye to them in the church parking lot and go home to take a nap. Parents, on the other hand, have to suffer with these sleep-deprived terrors until they are rested enough to be civil again. Our credibility falls when we end our events with kids who are zombies or gremlins.

Most parents prefer that their kids come back from events alive and unmaimed. Serendipitous cliff diving, drag racing with the church bus, and other acts of macho heroism will all be lauded by the kids. Rest assured, however, they'll come home and expand the truth to tell an even more exciting story. Rest assured, also, that this will not play well with the parents.

Carl, a new youth worker with junior highers, thought he'd give the kids a little thrill while heading home from a camping weekend. Driving the church bus on a mountain road with a drop-off on one side, he accelerated when he saw a sign that said, "Caution, Dip, 10 mph." The dip was actually a washout—five feet steeply down, twenty-five feet level, and then five feet steeply up. Behaving more like an F16 fighter pilot than a bus driver, he hit the washout at 35 mph. The kids in the back of the bus were thrown from their seats nearly to the ceiling. Those who'd been napping found themselves on the floor. Suitcases and sleeping bags rained from the luggage racks. Kids roared with approval, chaperones (having just aged a decade) silently thanked God they were still alive, and Carl beamed in acknowledgment of his oh-so-cool macho-ness.

It was all pretty funny until the pastor's phone started to light up the next day with phone calls from parents registering their dismay.

Funny thing—parents also prefer that their kids not be given opportunities to become sexually active on youth group outings.

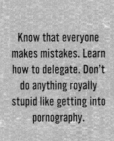

Know that everyone makes mistakes. Learn how to delegate. Don't do anything royally stupid like getting into pornography.

(FIRED, PRESBYTERIAN, SUBURBAN MISSISSIPPI)

My heart sank the day after a backpacking trip when I heard that a bunch of kids had shared tents and sleeping bags the last night of the trip. I heard this news from an angry parent.

A medical emergency had left one of our three hiking groups without adult supervision for one night. Since the group knew we had a long and difficult hike out the next day, I assumed they'd go to bed after our closing worship service and get a good night's sleep. Well, they went to bed, all right.

Back on the home front, if anarchy rules the Sunday school classroom, the parents will know. Not only will they know, but they'll question why we're letting it happen. I know of at least two cases where "lack of control" was the main reason certain parents crusaded for the youth pastor's removal.

## 2. Teaching and Advice

Some parents care, and care very deeply, about our counsel and teaching. They'll quiz their sons and daughters about what we teach in class and what we discuss during personal visits.

"Pastor Kageler, did you really tell my daughter to keep dating Chris, even though we don't approve?"

"Well, er, uh..." my mind replayed (at triple speed) my conversation with Sandy from the day before. This particular parent, for whatever reason, had always seemed unhappy with me. Fortunately, my stock in her eyes went back up to zero when I assured her I would call Sandy within 24 hours to clarify, since she must have misunderstood something I'd said.

It is important to think through any counsel we give kids. It's especially important when the issue is parent/teen relations. If we are in an evangelical church, our teaching better have some solid biblical foundation.

> We fired Fred because he was off-base and unbalanced in his teaching. He was always into prophecy—setting dates, identifying world leaders with specific Scriptures, that sort of thing. We talked to him about it, but it just got worse and worse. Then he became convinced the world would end on a certain week when all the planets were lined up in a certain way. He told the young people they shouldn't bother going to school, just stay home and pray. He stayed home too—didn't show at the office all week. Well, the world didn't end, but Fred's job did. There's more. His wife left him a few weeks later. Guess it's hard living with a prophet.

# KIDS: ON YOUR SIDE UNTIL...

Yes, we might experience some conflict with youth, too. Four percent of youth pastors who have been fired name conflict with kids as one of the reasons. Many more of us experience verbal or volitional collisions with kids at least occasionally. There are four areas to watch out for.

## 1. Not Being Like Your Predecessor

When you begin a new ministry, it's normal that you take someone's place. The old youth pastor has left, and you're the new kid on the block. Change is hard for young people in the youth group. If they liked the last youth leader, you're guaranteed to run into conflict if you're very different. Furthermore, if they nearly worshiped your predecessor, you can figure many of the current ninth through twelfth graders are a lost cause. Focus on the seventh and eighth graders—they don't have so many cherished memories. I learned this the hard way in my first church after seminary.

My predecessor's name was Matt. He was a virtual deity in the minds of many of the young people. Matt was a 75-hour-a-week youth pastor. He was *always* with them—always available for a pickup game of basketball or volleyball. On Thanksgiving and Christmas afternoons, he was at the church gym with the kids. His first child was born while Matt was on a youth event. This guy ate, drank, slept, and breathed youth ministry. His wife apparently didn't mind. The church board asked him not to work so much, but Matt paid no attention.

I began my ministry there seven days after Matt's farewell service, and three days after the youth group had tearfully helped him load the moving van. Unfortunately for me, I was a 55-hour-a-week youth man, not 75.

For 18 long months, not a day went by when I didn't hear some story about how great Matt was or how he'd done this or that. Seeking to avoid pain, I naturally gravitated toward the junior high kids. They had liked Matt too, but at least he wasn't a god to them. I found special comfort with my nerdy seventh-grade boys...I felt like a nerd, too. My breakthrough came when we did a junior high musical that the whole church thought was excellent. In the remainder of my three years there, even the older kids figured out how much I loved them, and they let me express it in my own ways.

My farewell service was a tearjerker, and we cried again while loading the moving van. Kurt came after me, and 18 months later *he* was finally out of *my* shadow. And that's about how long it takes to win the hearts of kids who dearly love someone else.

## 2. Changing Cherished Programs

We have our plans and programs in youth ministry. In our first few years, we'll no doubt change a program, a structure, or a way something is done. And that can sometimes lead to conflict.

If we are unlucky enough to be in a group that needs to be divided—say, junior high from senior high, or senior high from college—watch out: Conflict is coming. Boards may agree the change is necessary, parents may be all for it, but watch out because *one* group of people will fight us all the way. Usually, it's the kids just below the cutoff line—particularly the girls. Eighth-grade girls will fight to stay with the ninth to twelfth graders, and twelfth-grade girls will be desperate to remain with college kids.

Are the kids so ministry-minded they resent a narrowing of their mission field? Not exactly. Yes, they come unglued because their field is narrowing—but it's not the mission field as much as the dating field. Eighth-grade girls aspire to eleventh-grade boys, not 13-year-olds. Sweet 17s lose little sleep about their chronological peers, but dream about being with college guys or even older.

## 3. Rules and Regulations

Valiantly, we attempt to please parents and pastors by eliminating anarchy in our classrooms, youth programs, and retreats. In doing so, we win the respect of most kids, too. But not all.

According to James Dobson, 21 percent of those in any youth group will be *very* strong-willed. [1] Among these will be a good number of kids who are the second-born child in their families. According to those who do birth order research, second-borns like rules and structure about as much as cats like showers. Many strong-willed or second-born kids are heavily influenced by peers and like to push authority to the limit.

Strong-willed kids may enjoy hearing our rules and expectations, because breaking these rules provides them with a new challenge. In some cases they may choose to be passive, but their body language will scream defiance. If they're not passive, we'll notice—no doubt about it. As we begin our first months and years of ministry in a new location, we can expect the strong-willed kids will find ways to test our limits and gauge our reactions. This may bring us into conflict or, if handled well, it may not.

I remember my first church family retreat. I had a room full of ten boys, and I told them how much I'd looked forward to this time with them. We stayed up very late, then I explained to them it was now time to get some rest. I really stressed the need for their cooperation—it was already 2 a.m., and I expected them to go to sleep.

I came back from brushing my teeth and immediately had the strange sensation I was alone. Yep...my room was empty and the back door was open to outside. I closed the door, turned out the light, and went to bed.

About an hour later the boys "snuck" back into the room, barely disguising their glee. They wondered aloud how I could be so soft as to let them get away with it. There I was, sound asleep! The next morning I greeted them all pleasantly, and by breakfast time they were convinced they were in the clear. At breakfast I made the following speech to the whole retreat: "I really have enjoyed my cabin of boys, but I want them to know that all this is a privilege, not a right. Last night, my boys lost the privilege to have their own cabin, so tonight they'll get to sleep with their parents."

Dutifully, and with much remorse, the boys moved their stuff out after breakfast. The retreat and my relationship with the boys went great. I later heard they would privately coach newcomers on retreats with the words, "Len loves to have fun; he's great. But when he gives a rule, he means it. Don't cross him, or you'll pay."

## 4. Surprise! If We Don't Like Them, They Won't Like Us.

Young people give respect to the *person* in authority, not the position. If there ever was a day when young people had the attitude of "touch not the Lord's anointed," it has long since passed into oblivion. We have to earn the right to be heard. We have to earn the right to be respected.

Actually, this is one of the things I enjoy most about ministry with junior high youth. Each new crop of sixth graders cares nothing that I teach youth ministry or write books. All that means *zero* to them. What they want to know is: Do I love them? Can they trust me? Am I real? If we don't answer those questions right for our youth, we're in for trouble that could cut short our ministries.

> We fired Kent because he had the gift of guilt. Whenever he was up front, he was trying to make the youth feel guilty. He didn't talk to them personally, and showed little interest in them. He loved to lead things, and have kids obey his commands. It was like he was on some kind of power trip or something. If he could make a kid look foolish, it made him look better—or so he thought. Parents called us on the board to say that their kids didn't want to go to youth events anymore. My kids gave up on him, too, and they're normally really supportive.

Conflict, conflict everywhere. It's easy to get discouraged. As we look toward years of ministry ahead, it may seem like we're tiptoeing through a minefield. Yes, there will be conflicts. No, they don't have to ruin us or our ministries. Be patient, we'll get to the positive solutions soon. Remember, we are first trying to get a picture of the hazards ahead in ministry. We've looked at conflict: now we need to look at compromise.

# COMPROMISE (OF THE MORAL KIND)

When I teach about moral compromise with my "Intro to Youth Ministry" students here at Nyack College, many of these freshman students, age 18, assume I'm going to speak about helping *youth* avoid moral compromise. But that's not what I'm talking about. I'm talking about helping *you* avoid moral compromise. And, in particular, I want to talk about helping you avoid compromising your *sexual* morality.

Many of my students have never considered the possibility that a good Christian youth worker would ever find any kids in his/her youth group sexually attractive, or that good Christian young people would ever see their youth pastor as an object of sexual desire or conquest. Many have never thought about the temptation some married youth workers feel in sexual attraction to other youth workers on a youth ministry staff.

If you read the Preface of this book, you know it is a revised and updated version of a book I wrote fifteen years ago. One very real difference between the results of the study I did while writing the first book and my more recent study had to do with moral/sexual compromise. Back in 1992, over 20 percent of the youth pastors who were fired lost their jobs due to sexual misconduct. My 2006 survey shows the rate of sexual misconduct has dropped to 6.4 percent. Though this is still too many, the improvement is great news. I'd like to think there's been positive change as those who speak to youth workers have become more open about the issues.

Let's be honest. If you're a male, you think some of the girls in your youth group are gorgeous, right? If you're a female, you see some of the guys in your group as gorgeous too, right? There is nothing wrong with admitting this. One time I was on a school campus and one of the girls from our youth group saw me enter the courtyard. She yelled, "Len!" then ran through a crowd of 100 students (who were all now watching) and threw her arms around my neck, nearly knocking me over. Yes, my heart rate quickened, and it wasn't because of embarrassment. A youth ministry veteran once confided to me, "Sure, I'm attracted to some of the girls in my group, and now the problem is even worse—I'm attracted to some of their mothers, too."

Attraction itself isn't wrong; it is very normal. What matters is how we respond to it. When not handled properly, these can become *fatal attractions* for our ministries. Here are some examples from the survey:

> He was married but too forward with some girls. He charmed them, but this made others feel uncomfortable. Things finally caught up with him.

> Sexual impropriety with several girls in the group after his marriage fell apart.

> He made inappropriate comments to some girls. It looked like to the girls, and their parents, he was trying to seduce these students. After he was dismissed, we learned he was fired from his previous church for this, too.

> Our youth pastor is in prison now. He claimed he nearly finished med school and if a girl in the group had pains or other problems his "ministry" involved a physical examination and often sexual relations. It was bad enough for how it damaged some of the young people in the group. And when the news media got wind of this story...

> Our youth pastor didn't have sex with kids in the group, but he became addicted to pornography. His life totally fell apart because of it.

We'll consider some of the things we can do to guard against moral compromise later in the book.

Some youth workers are forced to leave their ministries due to conflict or compromise. Others leave of their own accord, due to burnout. But what does burnout look like?

# CHAPTER 4

# RECIPES FOR BURNOUT

"Wake up, Dad!"

I opened my eyes to three pairs of young eyes staring at me. I'd been playing with blocks/Legos/My Little Ponies with my three young daughters and had laid down on our carpeted floor to get a little pony perspective on the scene. I don't recall falling asleep, only waking up to my imploring daughters.

Unfortunately, this was not the first involuntary sleep response they'd experienced with me in recent days. Eventually, it occurred to me: "I'm on the road to burnout."

When we're really good at something in youth ministry, the church will often find a way to "maximize our strengths" by adding to our responsibilities, even if only "temporarily." If we're great at counseling, our sensitivity and insight may eventually be sought not only by youth, but also by their parents, by other people in the church, by the friends of other people in the church...you get the picture. If we're gifted in music and worship leadership, there will be ample "opportunities" offered (or assigned) to us where we can use these gifts. "Say, wouldn't it be great if you could head up the children's choir for Vacation Bible School. And how about the Christmas Program, the Easter Outreach, and of course, the children's special music for the Mother/Daughter Tea in May."

We may like these new responsibilities, and it's great to feel useful. But if we say "yes, yes, yes" without reducing some other aspect of our responsibilities, we set the stage for burnout.

No one in my church is tempted to ask me to counsel or lead music—I'm truly awful at both of these. But when it comes to mission and vision, leadership, and management, that's where the "add-ons" tend to come to me. When one church I was serving as youth pastor lost its senior pastor, the preaching was subcontracted to others, and I was made the "CEO," leading the governing board and the nominating committee, running the Annual Meeting, supervising the pastoral staff (five others), tracking church finances—that sort of thing. I was excited at first, because this stuff comes to me easily, like breathing. But I was not smart enough to realize that I had to reduce my youth ministry leadership and involvement if I were to take on these other tasks. Before long I was falling asleep while attempting to be a good father to our three daughters.

Most youth pastors don't begin ministry with burnout issues on the radar. They're fired up, not thinking about what might eventually quench the flame. But down the line all too many youth ministers experience feelings of discouragement, spiritual dryness, frustration, and a lingering weariness—the telltale signs of the soul-sapping drain that is burnout. One can hear such pain in the words of many who filled out my survey.

> Make sure you have a great relationship with your pastor and your pastor's family. Aim for a mutual respect, and always remember that you don't know everything.
>
> (FIRED, HOLINESS, SUBURBAN NORTH CAROLINA)

I got very tired and just couldn't do it anymore. Kids were always at my house.

There was no time left in the day for anything. Too many balls in the air. I got to the point I didn't care about God or church or anything. I just felt like walking away from everything.

---

I couldn't keep my head above water. Kids and parents were so critical of just about every decision I made. I couldn't help but take the burden of this home with me. I thought about it all the time, and I was no longer a real person.

---

I couldn't keep spiritually fed at my church, and there was no one my age to hang out with.

Of those youth ministers who were not forced to leave but left of their own accord due to burnout, here are the top reasons (respondents could choose up to 4 of the 12 listed on the survey):

| | |
|---|---|
| 1. PASTOR HARD TO GET ALONG WITH | 43 PERCENT |
| 2. FELT ISOLATED OR LONELY | 43 PERCENT |
| 3. SPIRITUAL DRYNESS, UNFED SOUL | 39 PERCENT |
| 4. STRAINED FAMILY RELATIONS | 36 PERCENT |
| 5. CRITICISM | 35 PERCENT |

The first step in rising above the issue of burnout is to understand what leads to it. (And take heart, we'll address some answers in due time!) Let's take a look at each of the top reasons for burnout.

# PASTOR HARD TO GET ALONG WITH

What does this look like? Hear some of the voices from the survey.

My senior pastor was an extreme micromanager.
I couldn't stand it any longer, his looking over my
shoulder about everything and trying to control
my day-to-day life.

My pastor was mishandling church funds. Some of
us knew but no one stood up to him or called him
to be accountable. I couldn't continue there and
keep my own conscience clear.

The senior pastor was insensitive and
manipulative. No one would stand up to him. Our
youth pastor eventually got so tired of seeing
this. Pastor was very condescending to the youth
pastor and about youth ministry.

Of course, youth pastors aren't the only ones who sometimes
have discouraging problems with a boss. In a Gallup Poll-based
study of 80,000 managers, Marcus Buckingham found that the
number one reason people leave their jobs is because of difficulties with the person directly above them in the organization.[1]

Some youth pastors find that conflict with a senior pastor or
supervisor can contribute to another oft-cited reason for burnout...

# FELT ISOLATED OR LONELY

One youth pastor in our survey wrote:

> The senior pastor and I didn't see eye to eye.
> With our personalities being so different, it was
> difficult to work together. Our philosophies were
> different, and my wife and I felt very alone.

Feeling betrayed isolates us as well. Recently I spoke with a youth pastor who told me that he'd had some personal problems. Seth was glad there was a professional counselor who was on the church board, and he scheduled some sessions. He was stunned to later see, in a written report of the board, a specific reference to something Seth had told this counselor and no one else on the planet.

Here's how a few other youth pastors described their experiences of isolation and loneliness that contribute to burnout:

> I felt unprotected. My pastor never sided with me.

> She was in a high demand/low support situation. It became impossible for her to continue without bitterness.

> Too much to do, not enough time. I didn't have time for my own friendships. After a major public incident where a parent challenged my leadership, abilities, and morals, I began to feel very isolated. The church board half-heartedly tried to address the incident,

> I'm now part of a nationwide youth pastors' network that meets together once a year. Throughout the year we do conference calls. It's the greatest thing for any youth pastor who wants to make it to the end!
>
> (FIRED, NONDENOMINATIONAL, RURAL GEORGIA)

but the damage had already been done. My own sense of well-being was rocked and, because this person had a large extended family in the church, it seemed that everywhere I turned relationships were now strained. This led to loneliness, isolation, a feeling of hopelessness, and ultimately physical sickness. I just stopped making decisions; I couldn't handle the stress of choosing anything. I couldn't even order in a restaurant.

## SPIRITUAL DRYNESS, UNFED SOUL

Many of today's youth workers were not even teenagers yet themselves when Paul Borthwick wrote *Feeding Your Forgotten Soul: Spiritual Growth for Youth Workers.*[2]

Borthwick points out that there are many things that can drain spiritual life away.

For example, having the *wrong motives* for being in ministry is not conducive to spiritual health. I've met youth workers who seemed to be in it for control, or pride, or to become cool, or to have the fun they missed out on when they were teenagers themselves.

Another spiritual drain according to Borthwick is a *wrong definition of success.* Whenever we aspire to be the biggest or to have the best (whatever) in comparison to others, we get on a treadmill that can only wear us out spiritually and emotionally.

Excessive *busyness* is another soul killer. Yes, youth ministry is complex and multidimensional, but if we have basic self-management skills, the schedule and responsibilities need not overwhelm us.

The ache of the unfed soul was palpable among some of those who responded to the survey.

I lost my prayer life as a youth worker. There just wasn't time.

She just couldn't feel spiritually fed. Her pastor's sermons were hard to relate to, and the pastor gave no spiritual leadership or mentoring to his staff.

He was left to fend for himself spiritually while all that mattered to the church was increasing numbers at youth group. That was "fruit" to them.

## STRAINED FAMILY RELATIONSHIPS

Like many other youth pastors, I felt the stress of the ministry's impact on my family many times. My wonderful and supportive wife, whose giftedness and interests lay in other areas of church ministry, normally was not involved with the youth group directly. At our first church, where I was in charge of junior high, senior high, college, and couples—each of which had a weekly study I led plus other required activities—I was only home one or two nights a week. While I was free to come in to the office at noon if I wanted to, it just wasn't the same as having time together in the evenings.

When I interviewed for my second church, my first question to the board was, "What happens to me when the senior pastor leaves?" (Their answer: nothing. Good thing I asked, as the senior pastor resigned three weeks after my arrival.)

My second question was, "How many nights a week do you expect your pastors to be home with their families?"

Their answer? "Three or four would be about right—never less." I almost fell to my knees and begged them to hire me. I managed to maintain my professional demeanor, though, through the rest of the interviews. But when the official call came, I was quick to say yes before they changed their minds. One reason I stayed at that church 14 years is because the schedule was conducive to being a decent husband and father.

We can hear the pain over strained family relationships in many of the survey responses:

> He just couldn't get the balance between youth ministry and family. The bigger the ministry got, the more time he was away.

> I was working 50–60 hours a week and was out of town a lot speaking around the country. My wife had an affair with our first-grader's schoolteacher.

> My wife found it extremely hard to handle people's criticism of my youth ministry. I was usually able to forgive and forget quickly, but she just couldn't stop thinking about the criticism when she saw these people (some of whom were worship leaders) in each Sunday's service. This was very hard, then, on our relationship as a couple.

> My pastor had the idea that my low youth ministry salary was good because I was "paying my dues" and it would teach me to live by faith. I hung in there for many years but finally it occurred to me that as far as this pastor was

I think regular contact with other youth pastors is vital.

(BURNED OUT, ROMAN CATHOLIC, URBAN NEW YORK)

> Have a life outside your job. It's so easy to pour ourselves into our work and tell ourselves we're serving a higher purpose, but not even realize the emotional and mental drain we are causing ourselves.
>
> (FIRED, CHRISTIAN REFORMED, SUBURBAN NEW JERSEY)

concerned, my "dues" would never be paid. I felt bad for my family that there wasn't enough money for what was "normal life" for other people in our congregation.

## CRITICISM

I'll never forget it. It was the third week of my first full-time youth pastor job. There was a big backyard barbecue event with a good attendance of high school and college students. I was doing my best at mixing and mingling, still trying to learn names. I was feeling great; the youth seemed happy to be together; it was a perfect Vancouver, BC, early summer evening; I could see the snow-covered mountains to the north, rising almost straight up from the edges of the city. I was already looking forward to various backpacking trips and mountain retreats that were scheduled. I was jarred from my mountainous thoughts by the approach of someone I didn't know very well yet, Gerald.

Gerald had a different sense of personal space than I did. He stood with his face about six inches from mine and exclaimed loudly, so that all present could hear: "I think you've come to destroy everything Matt tried to create here!"

I mentioned Matt in the last chapter. He was the much-loved previous youth pastor at the church. I knew how highly they thought of Matt. But I was shocked that not one kid, not even leadership team students, challenged Gerald. Instead, I noticed some kids were nodding their approval. I didn't sleep very well that night.

Maybe they said something about this in seminary, but if so, I didn't get it. It had never occurred to me that people go through a grief process when they lose a pastor they've loved. Anger is part of the grief process, and some people seem to get stuck there for an extended time. It never occurred to me that I wouldn't be instantly liked. I assumed the "good ol' days of youth pastor Matt" would be happily replaced with the "good new days with youth pastor Len." It never occurred to me that it might take me many months (or years?) to be accepted and appreciated.

Remember the "Dear Pastor Kageler" letter that begins chapter 3? That counts as criticism too, no doubt about it. Criticism was certainly on the radar of many of the "burned-out" youth workers from the survey:

> The criticism I got seemed mean and unchristian. The parents expected me to fix their kids, babysit them, and make them into super-Christians. When it didn't happen to everyone, some parents were very vocal.

> Too much criticism from parents and students!

> Hard as I tried, I couldn't stop dwelling on the criticism. It was something that came to my mind no matter where I was, even on vacation.

Conflict, compromise, burnout—not a very happy list, is it? We've taken the time in these chapters to be honest about some of the potential downsides and difficulties of youth ministry. These kinds of things can cause even the most sure-footed youth pastor to stumble.

But don't be discouraged. Remember that we began the book with the ways youth ministry is worth the work and effort. Realize, too, that not every youth worker experiences intense conflict or withering criticism. In fact, many seem to sail through the ministry years with hardly a squall in the weather map. Some of this "smooth sailing" has to do with one or more of the insights and proactives that follow.

So let's get beyond the things that can trip us up and cause us to stumble, and focus instead on learning to soar!

**PART TWO**

# LEARNING HOW TO SOAR

# CHAPTER 5

# PERSONALITY PLUS (YOURS!)

I'm always thankful when I'm given opportunities to lead seminars for youth workers. One seminar I like to offer is titled: "Understanding Your God-Given Personality as a Key to Being Set Free and Unleashed to Serve with Enthusiastic Joy."

My seminar title is a mouthful, but the basic idea is short and sweet: God has given us our personalities. We know from Psalm 139 that God designed us and this great design includes our whole being, not just our bodies. Understanding the strengths and weaknesses of our personality packages gives us tremendous encouragement. I've seen people light up like Christmas trees as they realize they can be glad about who they are instead of sad about who they aren't.

Understanding your own personality, seeing how that personality impacts those around you, and understanding the personality styles of others will give you huge insights in relating to other people, particularly in stressful or confusing situations.

## UNDERSTANDING YOUR PERSONALITY

Personality differences have been a subject of curiosity and speculation for millennia. Hippocrates began the labeling process 2,500 years ago in ancient Greece, and temperament theory still receives much academic attention today. A few decades ago it was fashionable to recognize personality differences as simply the result of upbringing and environment. Today, however, many researchers see a strong biological determinant in how our personalities are shaped.

We're different because we were created different. Why would God want people to be different? One doesn't have to be a theologian to understand that each believer has a different function in the body of Christ. The teaching of Scripture on spiritual gifts is clear about this. (See Ephesians 4, 1 Corinthians 12, and Romans 12.)

We see personality differences all around us. Each of my three daughters has a very different personality. The kids in my junior high group are amazingly different. So are the members of our volunteer staff. This is great! Some kids connect best with Anthony, some with Mike, some with Allison, some with me, and so on.

My favorite way of explaining personality differences is by using the labels *Lions, Otters, Golden Retrievers,* and *Ants*.[1] Each of these categories describes a different personality type:

*Lions* are leaders and can be aggressive. They like to make decisions and make things happen. They are wired to be confident about themselves and their decisions. They don't require much information to make a decision and don't need much feedback as to how they are doing a particular task.

> Stay within your giftedness, develop volunteers. Take that day off, a whole one!!
>
> (FIRED, CHRISTIAN AND MISSIONARY ALLIANCE, RURAL NEBRASKA)

*Otters* are the life of the party—fun-loving people-persons who love to make wide social contacts. They are spontaneous, dynamic, and feel energized when entering a room full of strangers.

*Golden Retrievers* are deeply relational and sensitive. They love to get inside the head and heart of another person. They love to care and be cared for. They love to listen to the deep needs of others.

*Ants* tend to be organized and analytical. They make decisions comfortably only when they have all the facts in front of them. They are hard workers who take pride in doing things the right way.

Most youth workers I've met are strong in one or two of these personality areas. In the survey respondents were asked to name the personality type that best described them. Here's what they said:

| | |
|---|---|
| LIONS | 25 PERCENT |
| OTTERS | 32 PERCENT |
| GOLDEN RETRIEVERS | 30 PERCENT |
| ANTS | 13 PERCENT |

To better understand these four personality styles, let's first imagine four different rooms—each filled with people of the same personality type.

First, let's walk into a room full of Ants. It's a quiet but happy room. Ants don't require a lot of social interaction. Some Ants will be talking quietly and seriously; others will be saying nothing at all; and some Ants will have a brought a book or laptop computer along to make the best use of their time. Ants are content without a party.

Now step into a room full of Golden Retrievers. The noise level is higher because these Golden Retrievers enjoy interacting so much. They are sharing, listening, and are very focused. They enjoy getting to know one another deeply. If the building were burning down, they might not even notice, since they are so in tune with listening to and sharing deeply with one another.

If you dare, now come into a room full of Otters. It's party time! In this room Otters are laughing, joking around, and clearly enjoying one another. Paper airplanes sail across the room and (look out!) someone brought a super-soaker. Otters love action and would rather not be alone. Otters feel responsible for helping everyone have a good time. They are driven, so to speak, to help everyone smile and enjoy.

Let's take a look now at the only room I hesitate to show you. It is the only unhappy room of the four. You see, Lions are uncomfortable until they figure out which of them is the main Lion. Until that is sorted out, there can be some terse exchanges, attempts at one-upmanship, and verbal sparring to see who gets to be leader of the pride.

It is not hard to see how people of these four personality types differ when it comes to job satisfaction. Lions are happiest when in charge of something or someone. They like to manage, give orders, and make decisions. Otters make great salespeople. Don't put an otter behind a desk for long because she or he will long to be out with people. Ants make great accountants, actuaries, programmers, library acquisition personnel, and technical writers. Facing a day of minimal human contact is no problem to them! It's energizing, not draining. And Golden Retrievers make great customer-service representatives. You call up angry, and they make you feel as if they've been waiting all day just to listen to your pain and inconvenience. I once made just such a call about my Ford Taurus (which now has passed on to glory), and the Golden Retriever on the other end listened to my pain, acknowledged my frustration, and kindly let me know the Ford Motor Company wouldn't do a single thing for me. Despite the bad news, by the time the conversation was over, I actually felt good about the call and Ford. At least they heard my pain!

> Learn the personality of your church and its leadership. Be very diligent in communicating EVERYTHING to the proper people or committees.
>
> (FIRED, BAPTIST, RURAL NORTH CAROLINA)

Getting the picture? Let's talk about love. Sociologists enjoy this stuff when it comes to attraction studies. Lions and Otters tend to marry Golden Retrievers or Ants. It happens all the time. Lions find the sensitive Golden Retrievers so mysterious, so unfathomable, and so alluring. Golden Retrievers, on the other hand, are amazed by the confidence, direction, and outspokenness of Lions. Unfortunately, what seems so mysterious and wonderful in the warm glow of pre-honeymoon attraction can be downright irritating a few years later. (Computer-based matching services, such as eharmony.com, are largely personality-based. Their premise is this: People who are more similar have a vastly better chance of finding joy, fulfillment, and a lasting marriage.)[2]

Do we find these creatures in the Bible? Well, yes and no. No, these four personality types are not listed along with the gifts of the Spirit. But yes, we certainly see personality differences in the Bible. Paul and Peter are very Lion-like. Was Andrew an Otter? Friendship evangelism has been called *Operation Andrew* by the Billy Graham organization. How about Mary and Martha? Luke 10 portrays Martha as the organized Ant, and Mary as the soak-it-all-in Golden Retriever. I think Nehemiah, who supervised the re-building of Jerusalem's wall against impossible odds, was a combination of Lion/Ant. There's a combination that can get something done!

We've looked at these four personality tendencies from several different angles. Now let's make the leap to youth ministry.

## GOOD NEWS FOR ALL TYPES

Before we think about how personality type might relate to the firing or burnout of youth ministers, let's start with the positive. It is encouraging to know that God uses all kinds of people in youth work! His calling is not limited just to Lions, or just to Golden Retrievers, or any one type. If we think about Jesus' selection of the Twelve, we are reminded that he chose disciples with a variety of personalities who would eventually be let loose to turn the world upside down.

Let's consider the strengths of each personality type as it pertains to a vital youth ministry.

*Lions* have no hesitation about standing up in front of the group. After all, someone has to be up there, right? If not a Lion adult, then a Lion kid can be comfortable being in charge. Many people fear speaking in front of others more than they fear death itself. Well, Lions don't have this problem. Lions are great at providing direction, vision, and a sense that the youth ministry is going places. They don't get bogged down with decision making. It would not take a Lion long to decide whether to do an evangelistic mission trip, help build a house with Habitat for Humanity, or both.

On the other hand, I once overheard one end of a 45-minute phone conversation between two Golden Retrievers who were trying to decide what to do that evening. It was clear that each of them wanted to be absolutely sure the other was happy and that the other's needs were being met. Lions don't feel the need to approach decision-making with such caution and care. They say, "Let's decide, let's go, and let's get it done!"

There is much in a Lion that is attractive to teenagers. Kids like a sense of purpose and direction. They want meaning. Lions are great when it comes to "telling it like it is" and leading youth into meaningful challenges in which kids experience for themselves the joy of making a difference. Parents and church leaders tend to have confidence in a ministry led with vision and purpose

I have in front of me a 500-page text titled *The Sociology of Leisure*. Well, Otters don't need a book like this to understand fun! Otters want to have a good time, but their desire is not selfish—they want others to have a good time as well. In youth work, Otters are the kind of people who make kids smile, laugh, and go home exclaiming, "That was awesome!" Otters love to have fun, be it a spontaneous trip to Pizza Hut or a carefully planned Jell-O wrestling outreach event.

Otters make great youth workers because they want to make sure every single kid who walks in the door feels at least a little bit good. Otters work hard to create a positive atmosphere that attracts youth and makes them feel comfortable. Kids are attracted to Otters because they're attracted to life. An Otter-led youth ministry is one in which youth feel good about the group and their involvement in it. They enjoy bringing friends because they know their friends will have a good time and hear a positive message.

Of course, youth ministry isn't the only place in the church where personality has significant impact. The church I attend recently welcomed a new senior pastor. My wife and I have attended this church since 1994, and our previous senior pastors have included one Golden Retriever, one Lion, and one Ant. Now we have our first Otter senior pastor, and in only three months the church has been transformed. The church and its worship services have a new positive energy. Our pastor smiles when he preaches (the Lion tended to scowl) and sometimes tells stories in his sermons that are so funny we laugh hard enough that tears come to our eyes. Many people say they can hardly wait for Sunday to come, and they are eager to invite neighbors.

Youth ministry is a job made in heaven for Golden Retrievers. Adolescence is a stormy time, and it's rare when a kid doesn't feel insecure or hurting about something. Golden Retrievers are there for them! The gifts of time and an ability to listen are blessings that Golden Retrievers bring to youth ministry. They are concerned that the personal needs of young people are met.

Golden Retrievers are especially good at hanging out before and after a meeting or event. I have seen kids and Golden Retriever leaders standing around talking in the church parking lot long after the youth room is cleaned up, the lights are off, and the doors are locked.

Kids are attracted to Golden Retriever-led youth groups because they know they've got a friend. Programs do not bring people; people bring people. The connectedness kids feel to the Golden Retrievers in a youth ministry ensures their return again and again and again.

Ants can also make great youth workers. Ants are never sloppy in their organization, and the attention to detail shows in the quality of the ministry. Kids and parents know that if an event appears on the youth calendar, it's going to happen, and all the bases will be covered. The ministry is going to flow because the many details needed to run it successfully are both understood and handled eagerly by Ants. Ants keep people informed, they don't lose money, and their word is good.

Ants can be masters at one-on-one discipling, not only by mentoring in spiritual truth but through shared interests. I know Ant youth workers who find kids to share their hobbies. Fishing, model boat building, and remote control aircraft flying are great arenas in which the gospel can be nurtured in a young heart. Quality time is often a function of quantity time, and Ants are very creative in finding areas where time can be invested in building relationships with youth. Kids value the stability and trustworthiness of Ants. Youth appreciate the one-on-one time with a caring adult that's all too absent in many of their homes.

A few years ago, I did a study of the relationship between personality style and numerical growth in youth ministry. My survey of 500 youth ministries found that all types of personalities were associated with growing youth ministries.

## Percentage of Youth Ministries That Saw a Numerical Increase at its Main Meeting over the Previous Two Years

| Main Personality Type of Youth Pastor | Percentage of Middle School Groups That Saw Growth | Percentage of Senior High Groups That Saw Growth |
|---|---|---|
| ANT | 74 PERCENT | 48 PERCENT |
| GOLDEN RETRIEVER | 62 PERCENT | 54 PERCENT |
| OTTER | 66 PERCENT | 59 PERCENT |
| LION | 81 PERCENT | 69 PERCENT |

Although each personality type drips with potential for positive outcomes in a youth ministry, there is a downside to every upside. Our personalities, with all their God-given strengths, also have weaknesses.

Lions are "good" at being insensitive, causing people to feel their opinions don't matter, and making rash decisions. Otters don't need anyone to disciple them about how to be disorganized, poorly prepared, or lacking in follow through—after all, "it will all work out." Golden Retrievers may appear nervous in front of

20 noisy junior highers, and the paperwork required to run a full-fledged youth ministry can seem like a crushing burden to them. Ants won't attract many Otter youths since Ants find it difficult to project enthusiasm in the group setting.

In my years of being a youth worker, I've seen Lions get fired for being too stubborn. I've watched Otters pick up their last paycheck because their ministries lacked the necessary structure and organization. I've seen tear-filled Golden Retrievers crash and burn over the sustained criticism of one or two people. And I've observed Ants sent packing because too many church kids complained that youth group was boring.

## KEY INSIGHTS FOR NOT ONLY SURVIVING BUT SOARING

### Know Who You Are

I believe awareness of personality type is one of the two most crucial pieces of knowledge youth workers need to flourish. (The other key understanding relates to our own spiritual formation. We'll talk about that in chapter 8.)

Some may protest that personality typing is just another way to label people, and that labeling is a simplistic and possibly damaging way to understand people. I know that there are a zillion different personality profiles out there. (Okay, that's an exaggeration—Googling "personality tests" yields only 2.5 million Web sites.) I grant that people are complex and may behave in different ways in different circumstances. But there is significant evidence to indicate that personality tendencies are *hardwired* into us before birth, and this hardwiring has profound implications on individual human development. (If you are interested in the brain research side of all this, you may want to read *Galen's Prophesy*, by Harvard University's Jerome Kagan.)[3]

Knowing who you are and *being able to see yourself as you interact with others* (almost as if from above) has a great deal to do with success in life, no matter what the endeavor. Daniel Goldman calls this "emotional intelligence" and believes it (knowing yourself, seeing yourself) is vastly more important than "IQ."[4]

One great thing about knowing yourself is being aware of what you're good at. When we do what it seems like we were born to do, it's like we can hear God singing over us. As a Lion/Otter I'm good at creating a positive, affirming, fun environment. I'm good at leading leaders. I'm driven to affirm and build youth and youth workers. On the other hand, I'm terrible at counseling. Ask me to set up a six-session counseling session with a young person (or a parent) and my heart will sink. I'll dread every meeting. Ask me to have a deep conversation with a kid in need when there are 10 (or 50) other kids around, and it's like you're asking me to do the impossible. I'm so driven to meet/greet/make-feel-a-little-bit-good every single kid who comes in the room. Some of you are saying "Yes, that's exactly how I feel," while others are saying, "I can't believe he can't do what every youth worker *should* be able to do."

Speaking of *shoulds*...

> It's important to know you cannot do everything yourself. You have to have good people surrounding you to help you in all the areas of youth ministry.
>
> (BURNED OUT, ROMAN CATHOLIC, SUBURBAN CONNECTICUT)

## Realize Other Personality Styles Are Not Wrong, Just Different.

I nearly drove a godly and gifted youth ministry intern insane by my expectation that he meet kids at school during the week and take them to lunch. I took kids to lunch routinely. Most schools in my area had a 31-minute lunch break. I could pick the person up (if it was a girl, I'd make sure she brought one or two friends), take them to a nearby fast-food place, eat lunch, and have them back to campus with two minutes to spare. On the way back to school, I'd ask if there was anything I could pray for them about, and if the answer was longer than a couple of minutes we'd talk on the phone after school or in the evening.

My intern, Jim, told me over and over, with stress written all over his face, that he just couldn't have a 31-minute lunch with kids. For the longest time I just couldn't understand why he couldn't get with it, measure up, and get motivated to do this incredibly (to me) easy and simple task.

It finally hit me one evening after youth group when I saw Jim, as always, talking deeply with one or a few kids after youth group. I reflected on what he said was the best thing in youth ministry for him: "getting deep with kids." I finally had this epiphany: "Jim is different from me, and it's okay! He nearly wept with joy when I told him I no longer expected him to do lunch appointments, and that I was so happy he took the time to really talk deeply with kids.

Then I had another epiphany: Every one of my volunteers (there were 30 at the time) is wired to be very good at something. I should figure out what that thing is—and unleash them to do it.

Now perhaps this seems elementary to you, but for me, it was life-changing and ministry-changing. Ever since then I've asked all the volunteers and paid staff in my youth ministry to take this personality test. And then I've used the results to help them find areas of ministry where they will excel. I tried to make sure Lions were in charge of something from time to time. I had my Otters lead games and plan fun stuff on retreats. I gathered lots of Golden Retrievers, made sure they were in small groups with kids, and never expected them to stand in front of the youth group. And I made sure every Ant on the team had something administrative or detail-oriented to do.

As you might expect, people got very happy. They were being empowered, not enslaved in youth ministry.

I've had some good (and yes, even deep) talks with youth pastors about personality differences, and one thing often comes up: "If I do what you say, it will be obvious some kids will relate more closely with others than with me as the youth pastor. I'm tempted to be jealous when I see kids attracted to others, not to me." Yes, those feelings are real—but when we get past that pride issue and learn to rejoice when our volunteers are connecting with kids in ways we never could, our ministry can truly soar.

## Don't Quit Work—Network

The key to overcoming the weaknesses inherent in our individual personalities is networking. First, we need to network with God. There is nothing like a glaring weakness that forces us to get on our knees and acknowledge that God is our source of strength, hope, and effectiveness.

Recently, one of my junior highers poured out a personal crisis. He was in pain and he'd come to me for care. Internally I panicked—knowing that counseling was not one of my strengths. But as my spirit settled down, God was able to use me in this kid's life. I was weak, but in God's strength I was able to function.

You can bet your last Big Mac that this kind of spiritual exchange—exchanging our human weakness for God's strength—takes place thousands of times in ministries across the country every week. Lions find themselves in counseling situations, Otters are writing up the summer camp reports for the Elder Board, Golden Retrievers are leading the "shuffle your buns" game, and Ants are trying to keep 15 wiggly junior highers from climbing out of the windows during Sunday school. Indeed, with God's help we can achieve things we might never achieve on our own.

> We are not gifted in all areas of ministry. No one is. Let us bring our gifts to the church and bless the body of Christ, and be thankful for the giftedness in all God's people.
>
> (FIRED, NONDENOMINATIONAL, SUBURBAN PENNSYLVANIA)

Networking with God is crucial; so is networking with others in youth ministry. In other words, we have to think "team." We need people unlike ourselves working alongside us in ministry. Lions need Golden Retrievers to provide the personal care youth so desperately need. Otters are in critical need of Ants who can handle the details. Golden Retrievers need Otters and Lions who don't mind being in front of the group. Ants need Otters to create the positive and fun atmosphere essential to a growing youth ministry.

We will still sometimes find ourselves functioning in areas where we are not strong, but we thank God for his grace and for the others who are filling out the whole personality picture with us.

There can be amazing joy in all of this.

Recently, I had occasion to thank God for Golden Retriever Allison and how she puts her arms around those sixth-grade girls, making them feel so cared for. I thank God for Otter Mike, who tirelessly plays tag or basketball in the parking lot. I thank God for Ant Janet, a parent who eagerly keeps track of any retreat or event finances so others don't have to worry about it. And I thank God for Lion Marv, our youth pastor who confidently makes plans and gets everyone excited about what's ahead.

As we understand our God-given personalities, we are set free to serve him in enthusiastic joy.

# CHAPTER 6

# YOUTH MINISTRY, BEING MARRIED, AND HAVING A LIFE

"Well, that will be it then."

My good friend stood in the living room, having just returned late (as usual) from a youth event. His wife had one hand on the doorknob, her packed suitcase in the other. In wide-eyed amazement my friend asked, "What are you doing?"

"I'm moving in with my sister. The fact that you couldn't see this coming shows me again how lost you are. Obviously the promises you made when we got married meant nothing. You're not married to me; you're married to a bunch of teenagers." With that she opened the door, slammed it shut, and drove off into the night.

Ultimately, my friend and his wife were able to reconcile and rebuild their relationship. But the experience, as you can well imagine, was a mighty wake-up call for my youth pastor friend.

In this chapter we're going to take a hard look at balancing the demands of youth ministry with our private lives and our primary relationships. If things are not good on the home front, whether we are married or single, it's pretty hard not to crash and burn in the ministry. This is a subject that almost never comes up on the radar in most youth ministry books. Here, we will look at the problems and address some positive steps we can take to avoid these crises before they ruin us and our ministries.

Among those in our survey who named "burnout" as one of the main reasons for leaving a ministry, 42 percent of the respondents named "felt isolated or lonely" as one of the top reasons. "Strained family relations" was another top choice, mentioned by 34 percent. Here's what a few of them had to say:

I felt I was spinning out of control and couldn't find a way to stop.

The male single staffers at our church were treated like lost puppies...They were invited to people's homes for dinner, or food was often brought to them. They even had offers of help with laundry and housecleaning. As a single woman staffer I was almost never invited to a home for a meal and never did anyone offer to assist with something practical in my life. It was very hard not to be down about this difference of treatment.

He couldn't strike a balance between work and family.

I had no friends in the community. I had to be at church for Thanksgiving and Christmas and could never go where my parents and family were. People at the church knew this but didn't seem to care. I never was included in someone else's family holiday plans.

I felt like my family and I were living in a fishbowl.

# THE SINGLE LIFE AND YOUTH MINISTRY

Many people assume they will meet the person they are going to marry while in college. While this is true for some, it is not the experience of the majority. This means many who go into youth ministry after graduation from a college or university will do so as single persons. Of course there are tremendous positives that accompany singleness in ministry, affirmed by the Apostle Paul himself in 1 Corinthians 7:32-35. There are, however, some downsides as well.

## Loneliness and Isolation

There is a dramatic difference in the "isolated/lonely" experience of youth workers based on marital status. Of the 350 survey respondents 75 percent were married, 25 percent single. In the survey 12 possible reasons for burnout were given and respondents could choose up to four reasons. Among those who chose "feeling of isolation or loneliness" as a reason for burnout, some real differences appear.

First of all, 65 percent of the single persons in our survey listed "feeling of isolation or loneliness" as a reason for burnout, while only 35 percent of married persons listed this as a primary factor.

The feelings of isolation were especially extreme for singles living in nonurban contexts—either in the suburbs or (especially) in rural areas. Consider these figures:

## Percentage of Respondents Listing "Isolation or Loneliness" as a Cause of Burnout

|  | Single | Married |
| --- | --- | --- |
| URBAN | 50 PERCENT | 25 PERCENT |
| SUBURBAN | 62 PERCENT | 41 PERCENT |
| RURAL | 100 PERCENT | 25 PERCENT |

To say it another way: A single youth worker living in Cody, Wyoming; Pumpkin Center, South Dakota; or Hop Bottom, Pennsylvania is far more likely to feel lonely or isolated than a single in Seattle, Atlanta, or New York City. Also, all singles are far more likely to feel this isolation than married youth workers, no matter where they live.

Of course personality plays a big part in the experience of isolation and loneliness as well.

## Percentage of Single Persons of Each Personality Style Who Named "Isolation or Loneliness" as a Reason for Burnout

| | |
|---|---|
| LIONS | 44 PERCENT |
| OTTERS | 66 PERCENT |
| GOLDEN RETRIEVERS | 81 PERCENT |
| ANTS | 40 PERCENT |

The Lions and Ants among us don't require nearly as much ongoing human interaction and connection as do the Otters and Golden Retrievers. An Otter youth pastor ministering in rural New Hampshire told me recently that he gets very tired of playing video games in his apartment—even online playing with others gets old in a hurry.

So what's the solution for a single youth worker who feels these pressures? We can't all move to Seattle, Atlanta, or New York City where dynamic, huge churches filled with 20- and 30-somethings abound. What options do singles have to cope with the dangers of loneliness and isolation?

Having a *small group/accountability group* is key. In some case, there may not be enough like-aged people within 100 miles to form a group that can gather in the same place regularly, but with

A well-balanced life is a must. It is so easy to get caught up in ministry. It will consume you 24/7 if you do not put limits on it. No one else is going to tell you not to work so much and take care of yourself. Sadly, the church will take full advantage of someone if he or she allows it.

(BURNED OUT, ROMAN CATHOLIC, URBAN GEORGIA)

great cell phone plans and the Internet, it's possible to meet virtually if not physically. This, of course, requires time. My New Hampshire friend spends at least an hour a week on the phone with his accountability partner. They don't only talk about the serious stuff of youth ministry and life's deeper issues, they also laugh over YouTube videos, discuss movies, and recap the recent week's football games. Such relationships are essential.

*Conferences and conventions* can be lifesavers. There is an amazing lift that comes with worshipping with 1000-5000 other youth pastors. Many denominations have youth worker support networks, and there are often regional youth worker gatherings operating under the umbrella of the National Network of Youth Ministries. We must choose to be with people like ourselves, and celebrate God's call on our lives.

*Communicating and negotiating with our churches* is important as well. Do they expect you to be working at the church on Thanksgiving, Christmas, and New Year's Eve? If you feel a need to be with family at holiday time, express your need. At least ask for a three-year rotation, where you'd have Thanksgiving weekend off one year, a week at Christmas the next, and a week at New Year's the next. Suggest it as an experiment—perhaps you and the church will find that the kingdom of God manages to lurch ahead even if you are not present at the Thanksgiving service every single year! It may be possible for you to raise this concern near the end of the negotiations as you prepare to take a new position. But watch out: If the senior pastor is a workaholic, chances are good that the church will expect you to be one as well. "Know before you go."

Additionally, it's okay to *admit life's learning curve.* Some new youth workers jump at the first job that comes along once they leave school. Perhaps they've never been far from home for more than a semester. Perhaps it hasn't occurred to them that post-college life is not filled with the constant presence of friends and spontaneous mall movies or late-night pizza runs. They're now in ministry and *wham*—the things once taken for granted that made life fun are now almost completely absent. Often we don't realize something is important to us until that something is missing. It's life's learning curve, and it's okay! Unless God has written your calling to a lonely place on a tablet and lowered it from the sky, it is okay to think about and pray about the context of your next ministry, and choose a situation that meets your needs. By God's grace you can do well in ministry in that lonely place, but we are wired to learn, and it's okay to make ministry location choices based on what we have learned.

Boundary issues are also important, and negotiating them can be especially difficult for single persons. Often the single life, particularly the young adult single life, is one in which the way we use our time is very flexible. We might find ourselves up until 2 a.m. playing an online video game against someone in Hong Kong, then sleeping late, grabbing breakfast at noon, running over to meet some kids for coffee after school, grabbing dinner whenever we feel like it, and then putting together the youth worship stuff (and rehearsing) at midnight in someone's basement. It's a great life, but especially with Wi-Fi and cell phones, we can *always* be working, wherever and whenever.

Henry Cloud and John Townsend have written a series of books called *Boundaries*. In a lifestyle where one is working, or able to work, almost 24/7, most people will eventually find themselves on the edge of burnout. One way to avoid this burnout-producing lifestyle is by setting a schedule. No, we don't need to program every minute of our time, but we do need to ensure there is a broad pattern of "time off" scheduled. Cloud and Townsend affirm that there must be some of our time where we are not working, so we can be refreshed and can recreate.

This balance of work and rest is mandated in Genesis. We were created to experience a cycle of work and rest. If we don't, we're messing with God's design for our optimal functioning.

We may think we are too busy, or our work is too important, to take time off. It is important to remember that "Sabbath rest" was a real leap of faith for those in the Old Testament. In a rural, agrarian economy, the work of planting and harvesting had to be done or one might not eat. To take a day off each week was a radical statement of faith, especially when the crops were not yet harvested and no knowledge of the ten-day weather forecast was possible. In the same way, our respecting the need to take a day off, even with youth ministry work undone or needs unmet, is a statement of faith that we believe God will enable us (or others) to get things done at another time.

> Keep your personal life separate from the church life. Don't make your identity a youth pastor; make your identity a follower of Christ. Your job is youth pastor.
>
> (BURNED OUT, PRESBYTERIAN, RURAL COLORADO)

I wish I could promise you that every church you'll work for will understand that rest and personal Sabbath time are essential for healthy ministry and will be eager to make sure your need for time away is respected. Some congregations recognize the importance of making sure the members of their pastoral staff get time away. But our churches are often filled with people who regularly live on the edge of burnout and overwork themselves. It may be up to us to guarantee that our schedules include the necessary personal time for rest and recuperation.

As a youth pastor I had marked Monday night as a time when I was "off." I considered this downtime to be a serious commitment—to my own health, to the vitality of my ministry, and to my wife and children. If Mrs. Smith from the missions committee called to say she wanted to have a meeting on Monday night with my presence to discuss youth involvement in the pending Missions Conference, I would say, "Hmm, I'm sorry—I have another commitment on Monday nights. Could we have the meeting Wednesday night before (or after) youth group, or Saturday morning, or Sunday night? Or perhaps you and I could meet some day prior to the Missions Committee meeting."

Not once, in my 20 years as a youth pastor, did one person ever say, "Well, just what is that Monday night commitment,

Len?" Some of them might have been surprised to find out that my commitment was to watch *Monday Night Football* and hang out with my family. And speaking of family...

## STAYING MARRIED AS A YOUTH PASTOR

The potential problems a career in youth ministry might pose for my own marriage came up right away at my very first church. Early on, my wife, Janet, helped me out with the youth, but we soon discovered (recall life's learning curve discussed above) that youth ministry was (definitely) not her area of interest and giftedness. One issue that brought us to a crisis point was that I was terrible at discipline/control with the youth group. Youth group was noisy, mostly chaotic, wild fun. She (as an Ant) saw long-term implications of the poor discipline in the group that I (as an Otter) couldn't see. Also, as an Otter, I gained energy as I stayed up late at youth events or on retreats, but she ran out of gas by mid-evening. She was eventually able to find other areas of ministry within the church that better suited her personality and gifts, and I discovered other (similarly Otterish) volunteers with whom I could party into the night—with or without the youth group. Ultimately, though, I missed her, and missed quality evening time just hanging out or finding free or cheap fun things to do together.

> Practice humility—the willingness to admit you're not perfect. Keep communication with the senior pastor continual.
>
> (FIRED, EVANGELICAL FREE, SUBURBAN NEBRASKA)

Many others have experienced this stress between marriage and ministry. I was really hit hard by these words of an anonymous author who wrote about her marriage to a youth worker in the pages of *YouthWorker Journal*:

> My husband is a full-time youth director. He is extremely dedicated and spends between 50 and 70 hours a week with young people.

I think the reason he is so successful with kids is that he is always available to them, always ready to help when they need him.

That may be why attendance has more than doubled in the past year. He really knows how to talk their language. This past year he would be out two and three nights a week talking with kids until midnight. He's always taking them to camps and ski trips and overnight campouts. If he isn't with kids, he's thinking about them and preparing for his next encounter with them.

And if he has any time left after that, he is speaking or attending a conference where he shares with others what God is doing though him. When it comes to youth work, my husband has always been 100 percent.

I guess that's why I left him.

There isn't much left after 100 percent.

Frankly, I just couldn't compete with God.[1]

I know I'm not the only one who has found it stressful to balance ministry with marriage and family life. My own 2006 survey showed that "strained family relations" was partially responsible for 36 percent of those who left their positions due to burnout. More than half of the respondents in an earlier study of 2,100 youth pastors by Strommen, Jones, and Rahn expressed concern about the impact of ministry on the amount of time they spend with their families.[2] Consider the responses to this item on the Strommen survey:

## My Family Gets Only Leftovers of My Time. This Concerns Me...

| | |
|---|---|
| VERY MUCH | 11 PERCENT |
| QUITE A BIT | 12 PERCENT |
| SOMEWHAT | 18 PERCENT |
| VERY LITTLE | 12 PERCENT |
| ONCE TRUE, NO LONGER | 16 PERCENT |
| NEVER TRUE | 31 PERCENT |

We see from Strommen's chart that while 47 percent of the pastors surveyed say family time is not a particular issue for them at the current time ("never true" or "once true, no longer"), for the rest time was an issue, and a critical issue for some. My own survey further highlights this as a big problem.

## Time, Youth Ministry, and Marriage/Family

Over my years of ministry, marriage, and then parenthood, I've learned my own time limitations and capabilities. For me, the comfort zone came in at around 50 work hours a week. That was pretty normal for other pastors I knew, plus very normal for most people in our congregations who are mid- or upper-level executives.

The stress my wife and I experienced over the time demands of my ministry decreased greatly when I instituted the "square system" of time use. Here's how it works.

Each week (Monday through Saturday) has eighteen squares — three squares each day, for morning, afternoon, and evening. We determined that each week should include six squares when I would be off. I knew myself well enough to know that feelings of unrest and frustration would begin to grow if I had less time off than this. Since I knew what meetings I had to attend on a regular basis, and we planned the youth calendar three to six months in advance, it was possible to mark my off-time several months in advance. So a normal "six-square" week for me might look like this:

|  | MON | TUES | WED | THU | FRI | SAT |
|---|---|---|---|---|---|---|
| AM |  |  |  | X |  |  |
| AFT |  |  |  | X |  | X |
| EVE | X | X |  |  |  | X |

Once these squares were marked on my personal calendar, I went home and entered the same information on our family calendar. This represented, then, my commitment to my wife and family. If friends phone our house wanting to get together, my wife knows when I am involved at church and when I am free simply by looking at the calendar.

Except for true emergencies—like a death or a family crisis that required immediate intervention—I would almost never change the schedule once it was entered on the family calendar. Keeping this commitment as a full-time youth pastor often meant that I would double (or even triple) schedule things on the nights I was working. Wednesdays were often like that. After youth group there might be an Adult Christian Ed meeting (also my responsibility) at 8:45 p.m. When that finished at 9:45 p.m. I might go out for ice cream or coffee with some of the volunteer staff (typically Golden Retrievers who were just finishing their "hang out" time with kids). Saturday mornings were usually triple-scheduled: breakfast with a kid, a youth leadership or discipleship meeting, and then a second kid appointment over lunch.

When there was a retreat or overnighter one week, I'd take a "comp" day the next week. It was an extra day off for recovery and family time.

Your tastes and needs for time use are no doubt different than mine, but the point is this: You need to figure out what you need. Obviously, this "figuring out" needs to include your spouse as well.

## Emotional Connection, Youth Ministry, and Marriage/Family

I was particularly struck by one comment from the anonymous woman I quoted earlier who wrote about her marriage in Youth-Worker Journal. Referring to her youth worker husband, she stated: "If he isn't with kids, he's thinking about them and preparing for his next encounter with them." A married youth worker who is only present physically while at home, but not mentally and emotionally, is setting the stage for burnout and marriage failure.

My wife seemed to have an innate sense of when my brain was too full of ministry things to genuinely pay attention to her or our children. We began to refer to this in computer language. How much of my RAM (random access memory) was still engaged in ministry and church issues when I was at the dinner table? At what point was my mental desktop too cluttered to pay attention to things that mattered at home? One thing that helped me was to imagine a line on the pavement about halfway home from church. Each day, when I crossed that line, I made a conscious effort to leave my work and ministry behind and shifted my thinking to home and what was going on there.

Maintaining an "emotional connection" to one's spouse is essential if a marriage would thrive and grow. The majority of youth pastors are men (76 percent in my study). Sociologist Brad Wilcox, in his book based on The National Survey of Families and Households, notes that women initiate two-thirds of U.S. divorces. Wilcox says that one of the most critical variables in determining whether a couple will divorce is the extent to which the wife feels a quality emotional connection with the husband. Said another way, this academic study concludes that a married woman is far more likely to want to stay married if she senses her husband is generally tuned in to her.[3] It is hard on the family when male youth pastors, eager to succeed (however success is defined), put all their emotional energy into ministry.

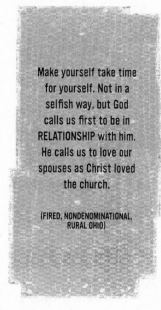

Make yourself take time for yourself. Not in a selfish way, but God calls us first to be in RELATIONSHIP with him. He calls us to love our spouses as Christ loved the church.

(FIRED, NONDENOMINATIONAL, RURAL OHIO)

Closely related is the whole idea of meeting each other's needs as a married couple. I have my senior youth ministry students read counselor Willard Harley Jr.'s book, *His Needs Her Needs*.[4] They are quite skeptical at first as to why they should read a book about building an affair-proof marriage. My reason is simple: If you are a youth minister and your marriage is in trouble, your ministry will eventually be in trouble, too. Most find the book very hard to put down once they begin, and they have to guard it from roommates and other friends "borrowing" their copy.

> Make boundaries with students—don't let them run your life. You don't have to be involved in every single activity. It's okay to tell kids and parents not to phone you on your day off.
>
> (BURNED OUT, EVANGELICAL FREE, SUBURBAN CALIFORNIA)

Harley says that we begin to "fall in love" when we find someone who makes us happy and makes us feel good. When we are with this person, it is as if deposits are being made into an internal bank. When the deposits get large enough, we are "in love" and want to make this arrangement permanent. Just as it is possible to make *deposits* in someone else's internal bank, negative things can be like making *withdrawals*. If there are too many withdrawals and too few deposits, if the internal bank account shows a negative balance for long, the relationship is in trouble.

One of the keys to building up that balance, to creating the foundation for a marriage that will last, is really getting to know the other person and his or her emotional needs. It's all too easy to "fall in love" and get married too soon before one really understands the other person. In the early stages of a relationship, we can sometimes fool our potential partner (and even ourselves) into thinking our interests are a perfect match. For example, if a woman wants to get to know a guy, she may become suddenly attentive to football, auto repair, and even the Xbox, as a way of connecting with him. The guy is thinking, "Oh my gosh, how cool is this??!!! I've found someone who likes to do the same things I like to do!" The reality, however, is that her interest in sports, cars, and gaming is just a (temporary) means to build a relationship. But the guy doesn't know this. He thinks he's found the recreational companion he's always dreamed of.

Guys are guilty, too. Sometimes I see couples at Starbucks, and I can tell they haven't been together for long. There he sits, hanging on her every word, absolutely focused, attuned even to the nuances of her body language. And his memory is so good. He really seems to understand her. She is thinking, "Wow, I've finally found a guy who really listens and understands me! How cool is this??!! Well, he's in the "getting to know you/falling in love" stage right now, but he may not be capable of a lifetime of long, intense, and deeply emotional conversations without end.

In the face of this, my students sometimes despair at the seeming impossibility of a good relationship. I urge them to go slow in dating, to be honest about themselves and their needs, and to make sure they are in a relationship long enough to have seen the real person—not only at their best, but also at their worst. A good marriage is one in which both spouses are seeking to meet the needs of the other, and such a relationship can give us the strong foundation that will help us endure the inevitable hard times of ministry.

## The Science of Love, Youth Ministry, and Marriage/Family

Most of us are familiar with Internet-based dating sites such as eHarmony.com, perfectmatch.com, and chemistry.com. Twenty-six percent (53 million people) of the U.S. adult population has either gone out with someone using one of these sites, or knows someone who has. Twelve thousand people a day fill out the questionnaire on eharmony.com.[5] Though these various Internet sites may ask different questions, they are all trying to do the same basic thing: discover "dimensions of compatibility."

The premise is profoundly simple, says Neil Clark Warren, founder of eHarmony. "In successful relationships, similarities are like money in the bank. Differences are like debts you owe. It is all right to have a few differences, as long as you have plenty of equity in your account." Sound familiar?

The relevance to youth ministry, marriage/family, and burnout is not hard to guess. A good marriage requires sufficient investment of time so that those "dimensions of compatibility" far surpass the differences. Early in a relationship, couples often do a lot of fun things together that build friendship and strengthen their shared interests. With job responsibilities and children, this time often gets squeezed out. Before long, there's no "money in the bank" and the normal stresses of life, including youth ministry, become harder to handle.

In the last two chapters we've laid a broad foundation that can not only keep us from stumbling but help us learn how to soar. If we understand the strengths and weaknesses of our own personalities and if we are taking positive steps as a single or married person to "have a life," we greatly reduce the possibility of becoming overwhelmed and overcome by some of the stressors of ministry.

Now let's take a look at how we can build positive connections with the other people who surround our ministries, particularly with the potential sources of criticism and conflict that the survey revealed: pastors/church leaders, parents, and the youth themselves.

# CHAPTER 7

# WORKING POSITIVELY WITH YOUR PASTOR AND OTHER CHURCH LEADERS

My senior pastor was very corporate. Our philosophies of how the church should run were very different. There were no angry words or arguments, it was just very apparent we were going different directions. My emphasis was more on discipleship, and his was more on getting bodies in the door. I was called into his office one day and was asked to resign. I believed he lacked integrity on how he communicated it to the congregation. They were led to believe I was resigning of my own free will so that I could move on to "bigger and better things." I was the third staff person "let go" in two years. I later learned he had a regular pattern of firing people under him. This was very rough on me, my wife, and my children, but we're in a much better situation now (great staff with great pastor!) and God has brought a lot of healing to our lives.

Having trouble with "the boss" is an all-too-common problem in the working world. The issue is sometimes more complex in youth ministry, because the youth minister's boss may be the senior pastor *and* the church board.

In our survey youth pastors who were fired were asked to choose up to three reasons (among ten) for their dismissal, while those who left due to burnout selected up to four (among twelve) reasons for leaving. "Conflict with the Pastor and/or Church Leadership" was named by 94 percent of those who were fired. Of those who left voluntarily because of burnout, 44 percent named the senior pastor as being "hard to get along with"—the number one reason cited. Obviously, the issue of conflict with church leadership is a big deal for youth pastors.

It's not surprising this should be the case. Our pastors and boards want a "successful" church. A successful church has to have a good youth ministry—everyone expects it. (Unfortunately, church members may have many different definitions of what makes for a "good" youth ministry!) When things go wrong in the student ministry, the church leadership eventually hears about it. Our senior pastor may hear about the concern before we do. The office of the senior pastor is a clearinghouse, an ecclesiastical funnel, through which bad news about us may pass. There may come a point when the quantity of bad news finally tips the balance against us, and we find ourselves in a major conflict.

It doesn't have to be this way. Many youth pastors enjoy great relationships with both their senior pastors and other church leadership. I've worked under five different senior pastors: one at my first church, and four at my second. (My third church had no senior pastor when I came and still had no senior pastor when I left.) Each of these pastors has been an excellent friend, and I thank God for them to this day. Not every youth pastor is as fortunate as I was. But initiative on our part can help make the senior pastor and other church leaders our allies instead of our enemies. In order to do that, there are three things we must do, by God's grace: first, understand them; second, have integrity ourselves; and third, build bridges.

# UNDERSTANDING DIFFERENCES IN MINISTRY PHILOSOPHY

To truly understand our senior pastor and other church leaders we work with, we must be aware of both their vision and philosophy for ministry as well as their individual personalities. Let's think first about vision for ministry.

I remember a staff meeting at one of my churches where differing philosophies of ministry became quickly and painfully apparent. We were evaluating the previous Sunday morning's service. All of us (we thought) felt it had gone very well. In recent weeks we'd had dozens of phone lines installed in the church, and church members had called 20,000 residents within a five-mile radius of the church building, inviting them to a special welcome Sunday. The "experts" had said 2,000 people would request more information about the church, and 200 people would actually show up on the special Sunday. And indeed, about 2,000 people requested more information about the church, and there were 190 new faces on the special Sunday. After discussing these numbers a bit, we were about to move on to the next agenda item, when one of our five pastors chimed in.

"But we didn't present the gospel."

"Well, Frank," our senior pastor replied, "we did try to interest people in becoming Christians, and those who are curious or hungry will come back."

"But there was no plan of salvation."

"There doesn't need to be," remarked another pastor. "We didn't have 'welcome Sunday' to give the impression we exist to jam the Bible down their throats."

"There should have been a gospel presentation and an altar call," Frank persisted. "The reason this church isn't growing is because we never present the gospel and ask people to respond."

Suddenly, the tension level in the room had gone from low to high, and a short agenda item turned into a long one, as a clear philosophy of ministry difference had been exposed.

A "philosophy of ministry" is basically a brief explanation of why and how we do ministry. Other terms often used include *mission, vision,* and *core values.* Thirty-four percent of those who were fired named a "philosophy of ministry difference" as one reason the dismissal took place—the third highest reason for firings. Many respondents went on to elaborate:

> My senior pastor had no philosophy of ministry, he never thought about it. He felt threatened when I tried to say we should have one.

> Conflict with pastor over postmodernism and new approaches to ministry.

> The church leadership was big on cheap grace—it was like you could just do as you pleased and God would automatically forgive. I believe we can't forget the cost to God but also what it costs us to be following Jesus.

How closely do you agree with your senior pastor and church leadership when it comes to issues of ministry philosophy? React to the following statements for yourself, and then consider how your senior pastor would respond. If you strongly agree, write in "10." If you strongly disagree, it's a "1." Scale the intensity of your agreement or disagreement accordingly.

(a) The pastors should dynamically lead the church rather than hanging back and equipping people to lead for themselves.

MY SCORE _____          MY PASTOR'S SCORE _____

(b) The sermon at the main service(s) should be prepared and given with non-Christians very much in mind. Christian growth and nurture is not the primary aim of this sermon; it should happen in other teaching settings in the church schedule.

MY SCORE _____          MY PASTOR'S SCORE _____

(c) Evangelism should be organized and structured by the church for its people, not left to happen haphazardly.

MY SCORE _____          MY PASTOR'S SCORE _____

(d) The sermon should be full of challenges and "oughts," rather than just trying to tell people who they are in Christ and what they have in him.

MY SCORE _____          MY PASTOR'S SCORE _____

(e) The worship service should be like a heavenly party rather than meditative and reflective.

MY SCORE _____          MY PASTOR'S SCORE _____

(f) The youth pastor and the senior pastor should have a close, supportive friendship.

MY SCORE _____          MY PASTOR'S SCORE _____

(g) The primary purpose of youth ministry is to reach lost kids, as opposed to nurturing and caring for kids already in the church.

MY SCORE _____          MY PASTOR'S SCORE _____

All this material is dynamite information—especially if you are smart enough to figure it out during the candidating process. You may also find it helpful to rank the items on the list by their importance to you. If you feel it is tremendously important that the Sunday service be fun, lively, and accessibly aimed at the non-believer, you're likely to have an upset stomach each Sunday as your pastor preaches through a year-long series on the book of Hebrews. If you feel it's essential that the pastor be a dynamic leader and he or she is a laid-back facilitator, you're bound to be in conflict.

The last item (g) proved to be a very oft-mentioned source of conflict among the survey respondents. We'll devote a whole chapter later to "Reaching the Lost without Frustrating the Found."

Of course, it is unusual that any youth pastor would agree with every view of the senior pastor or the members of the church board. In cases of disagreement, however, it is up to us to determine if we can live with the difference of opinion.

For example, in the church where I've been a junior high volunteer for over twelve years, the preaching style ("d" above) for most of that time was generally more "ought" than "are." Every Sunday we heard something else we ought to be doing more: praying more, giving more, coming more, being more dedicated, etc. We came to church and heard what we were doing wrong, and the ultimate message was, "You're not good enough. Do more." The way I'm wired, this is the absolutely worst preaching philosophy—yet I never left the church over it. My lifeline was a New York City church that made its weekly sermons available on CDs or MP3s, where the message was much more "are" than "ought." Those sermons about what it means when we live in Christ's strength and power spoke to what I most needed to hear, allowing me to continue to serve in the youth ministry. Now our church has a new

> Find a trustworthy person(s) whom you can go to for support and constructive criticism, prayer, and encouragement. Include the senior pastor in big decisions and always keep him/her informed.
>
> (FIRED, NONDENOMINATIONAL, URBAN WISCONSIN)

pastor whose sermons are much more "are" than "ought," and guess what? I can hardly wait to get to church when I wake up on Sunday mornings!

When it comes to understanding the priorities of our other potential boss, the church board, it's not hard to see what is important. Boards have the "big picture" in mind, or at least they should. Ideally, a church board works in partnership with the pastoral staff toward furthering the overall mission and vision of the church. We take a big step in understanding our church boards when we realize that what is most important to us may not be most important to them.

## UNDERSTANDING PERSONALITY DIFFERENCES

Once we understand personality theory and our own personality traits (remember chapter 5), it is much easier to understand the personalities of our senior pastor and even members of the board. If we have a Lion senior pastor, we can be sure, on the positive side, that she or he will be visionary, forward-thinking, and eager to get things done. On the downside, however, we probably won't receive a lot of personal care or mentoring from a Lion pastor. These traits are seldom on their radar.

One senior pastor I worked with was a Lion, and we got along great—since I have a lot of Lion in me as well. It was funny, however, watching some staff members interact with our Lion boss (whom we affectionately called "Dad"). "Dad" came to work regardless of his health; even the flu and a high temperature would not stop him from running three miles before breakfast and coming to the office to put in a full day's work. We had an associate pastor who was reluctant to come to the office if he felt *he might be feeling like* getting a cold. "Dad" just couldn't understand this caution.

If our pastor is an Ant or a Golden Retriever, we can be sure decisions for change won't come easy or quickly. Ants tend to hesitate to make decisions until every possible "what if" question can be thought of, analyzed, and answered with 90 percent assurance of successful outcome. Golden Retrievers value stability and consistency above nearly all else. They are not confident by nature, and are loath to make decisions that will cause anyone discomfort or have even a hint of risk. They're willing to discuss the issues for hours (months? years?), but have a hard time just moving forward with a decision. But on the positive side, Ants are fabulous at thinking strategically, while Golden Retrievers are tuned in to supportive friendships on the staff, and mentoring is as natural as breathing to most of them.

Of course, we are all complex people with a wide range of personality traits that come out in various ways and under various circumstances. I'm very grateful for the feedback I've been given about the impact of my own "Lion-ness" on the rest of the staff. Early in my ministry years I began to hear things like: "You make me feel terrible, because you are never down, never unsure, and it seems like you think you've never made a mistake. It would help me if you'd figure out some way you can show some vulnerability, because you make us feel like you're better than us."

Ouch! But I was—and still am—very grateful for those who have been willing to challenge me (like throwing themselves in front of a speeding bus) for my own good and the good of the ministry. One senior pastor I worked for (whom the staff called "Augustus") gave me this feedback with a follow-up assignment:

"Len, I know you have a list and a clock in your head 24/7. On Sunday mornings you're always rushing off to the next thing (and you often appear to be there mentally already), and you're ignoring people in the process. After the first service, I want you to STOP, just hang out in the sanctuary for 10 minutes, and don't rush to Sunday school. Just be there, standing in the sanctuary. After Sunday school, don't rush up here to the second service. Just STOP and hang out. We know you'll arrive and do your part; we're not worried about that. And after the second service, STOP..."

Ouch! I have to say this was a hard assignment for me (particularly since the ministry involved 250 kids, 50 volunteers, and 4 paid interns). But as the weeks went by, I found people coming to talk with me, almost surprised I was actually available. (I realize you Otters and Golden Retrievers are now thinking I was probably born on a different planet, if not in a different galaxy—but you fellow Lions know exactly what I'm talking about.)

When our pastoral staff and board members are all seeking to be filled with God and the fruit of the Spirit, we can help one another understand our own personalities and how we come across. If you are in such a situation, thank God! Over the years I've learned to appreciate the personality strengths of the people I work with, and the associated negatives that come with these personality packages no longer surprise me.

## INTEGRITY

A few of the respondents to our survey about why youth ministers burn out or get fired were senior pastors, who shared their own perspectives on why youth ministers were dismissed from their church staff. Listen to how one senior pastor explains the firing of his youth pastor:

> I asked the board to fire Brian because he was undermining my ministry as senior pastor. After being here just three months, he had a list of things about the whole church he wanted to change. He freely gave his opinions about my weaknesses to others in the congregation. He said I didn't have the right personality to lead a church successfully. I couldn't trust him anymore. He told some members of the youth group he wanted to be a senior pastor someday.

The confessions of an insecure senior pastor? Maybe. But if these charges are true, this youth pastor was behaving very immaturely. Integrity was lacking. What does it mean to have integrity as a youth pastor?

**1. Integrity Means We Understand We're Not Number One.** We must face this fact squarely and honestly. As youth pastors we are not in charge of our churches. The senior pastor has more authority. We do not have the last word. We do not have the final say. In fact, our great wisdom may not even be consulted on some churchwide issues.

Just like some of our don't-pet-my-fur-the-wrong-way young people, we may tense up when forced to accept the leadership of the head pastor. Were we "strong willed" as teenagers? Our past gives us clues about problems we may have now with authority.

Tony Campolo has observed three ways that youth pastors may try to do an end run around their pastors: 1) by displaying their more up-to-date education; 2) by casting the senior pastors as "keeper of the status quo," and 3) by using youth ministry to climb the denominational big-shot ladder.[1]

> Prepare a clear statement of ministry in advance of being hired. Identify your vision and be prepared to explain it. Ask questions about your job description to avoid "surprises" down the line.
>
> (FIRED, CHRISTIAN REFORMED, SUBURBAN ONTARIO)

To have integrity as youth pastors, we must abandon our craving for power and the games we use to get it. Yes, our education may be more recent than our senior pastor's. Yes, the senior pastor may be such a strong Golden Retriever that he or she seems unable to make decisions that will benefit the future of the church. And yes, if we're exceptionally good as youth pastors, we may find denominational or national recognition. But what matters is the state of our *hearts*.

Jesus clearly rejected the world's view of status and prestige. If we want to have his view, then we must have the attitude of a servant (Matthew 20:25-28). By God's grace and with his strength in us we must learn to be content where we are, in the position where we are now serving (Philippians 4:10-13).

I've struggled with this. Although all the senior pastors I've worked for have been good ones, and I've been a friend to each, two were especially weak in areas where I was strong. I'm a natural organizer. I plan things in my sleep and wake up in the morn-

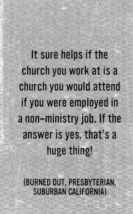

It sure helps if the church you work at is a church you would attend if you were employed in a non-ministry job. If the answer is yes, that's a huge thing!

(BURNED OUT, PRESBYTERIAN, SUBURBAN CALIFORNIA)

ing with some daunting project laid out in exquisite detail. I constantly felt frustrated with one of my pastors because he often had ministry problems that were the direct result of poor long-range planning, or no planning at all. (For example, he wouldn't even think about Easter until it was less than a month away, making any special outreach efforts impossible.) In my heart it was very hard not to "lord it over him" and feel smugly superior. God had to deal severely with my proud and hard heart.

Eventually, my heart was changed. With another senior pastor who was similarly weak in vision and leadership, I said little, focusing all my energy on the youth ministry. Eventually, he called me into his office and said, "It's obvious to me you've got a gift when it comes to vision and planning. I'd like you to tell me what we should do in this regard for the whole church, and I'll take it to the board. You do the dreaming, I'll carry it out."

Was I excited? Well…is water wet? Do birds fly? Is a venti skim quad-shot mocha with no whipped cream expensive? Sadly, my spirit soared for only a short time. A few weeks later this pastor was diagnosed with cancer and died some months after that. So we were never able to put this plan in action. But it was tremendous to a senior pastor who acknowledged and celebrated the strengths I brought to the staff.

**2. Integrity Means Avoiding Communication Quicksand.**
A second part of our integrity as a staff member deals with how we handle negative feelings about our boss and /or the board, both in ourselves and in what we hear from others.

If someone complains to us about the pastor or the church board, we must let that person know up front that it is not acceptable to complain to others without first talking directly to the senior pastor or members of the board. If the person who is complaining is misinformed, we may be able to set the record straight. But we need to avoid communication "triangles."

With regard to our own negative feelings, sensitivity is required. I've found that when I ponder the pressures my pastor is under, what's going on in his or her personal and professional lives, and his or her strengths and weaknesses, I usually decide to keep silent and just pray.

In one case I did decide to bring an observation to the pastor. I'd learned that the young people were ridiculing him because of a particularly odd and distracting gesture he often made while preaching. Later, he told me that at first he was very angry with me for telling him, but eventually he was grateful. By the way, he stopped using that gesture.

**3. Say Only Good in Public.** This final aspect of youth pastor integrity in communication is vital. There is good in every senior pastor. There are good people on every board. There is always something to praise, something to admire.

> If you find a place to minister where both you and your family feel loved and accepted, STAY THERE!!!! The grass may look greener somewhere else, but more often it's not.
>
> (BURNED OUT, CHRISTIAN & MISSIONARY ALLIANCE, SUBURBAN WASHINGTON)

It's nice when our boss has the same ideas we do. But it is important to offer public support for senior pastors and other church leaders, even when their ideas differ from our own. One senior pastor modeled this well when he told his new youth minister, "I want you to know that when we are in public, I will be behind you 100 percent...without exception. No matter what other people say to me about you, regardless of what you might have done, they will learn quickly that you are my man for youth ministry in this church, and that I am supporting you. Now, that doesn't mean that we won't have our differences and, privately, we may need to hash them out in a big way. But it does mean you can count on me to be your number one advocate in this church and in this community."[2]

A supportive senior pastor like this is a tremendous asset to any youth minister. (Anyone want to clone this guy?!) But it is essential that we offer that same kind of public support to others in leadership at our churches.

## BUILDING BRIDGES

One of my favorite meetings each month is the "Third Wednesday." About twelve of us in youth ministry gather over lunch to laugh, share, discuss, worship, and pray. Recently, we spent an hour talking about getting along with our pastors and boards. I took some notes. Here is a slice of that conversation:

*Kevin*:    For me it starts with prayer. I've got to pray for these people...all the pressures they face.

*Bonnie*:    Yeah, that's fine, but you gotta spend time together as a staff. Otherwise you won't even know what to pray about.

*Len*:    Our staff got a lot closer when we decided to take an hour each week outside of staff meetings just to pray for one another. That meant we had to be honest and get below the surface.

*Bonnie*:    I'll say again that the basis of good prayer, though, is relationship. Our staff goes on an outing about once a quarter. We might go for a day hike in the summer or out to a nice restaurant in the winter, that sort of thing. It's lots of fun.

*Steve*:    And with the board I communicate, communicate, communicate.

*Kevin*:    Which translated means...

*Steve*:    I've put all the board members on my monthly parent newsletter e-mail list. I also make sure they get the prayer list I give to our "parents in prayer" group each month. I make sure there's a written report from me in their board packet every month. I'm sure to be open about things that didn't go as planned as well as about successes. If I am asked to come to the board to give a verbal report, I do it with a PowerPoint presentation and throw in some pictures. I always—in every case—start with our student ministry mission/vision statement. They're starting to *get it*, I think. Oh, whenever I'm at something official with the board, I always dress professionally, and try to arrive a little early.

Kevin: Can I hire you to do this for me at my church, too? *(laughter)*

Len: Back on Bonnie's fun stuff. We tried a staff hike once. Our counseling pastor complained the whole way up and the whole way down. We've never let him live it down. His idea of an "outing" is to go outside and sit in a hot tub.

Bonnie: When I think the pastor preaches an especially good sermon, I tell him so. I appreciate the way he goes to bat for me at the board level, too. My husband is really into making pies (of all things!) and sometimes he makes the pastor an apple pie and we leave it on his desk with a thank-you note.

Steve: That sounds really cheesy.

Bonnie: But people like cheese!

Brad: I'm into cheesy, too. I've TPed my pastor's office with the help of some of the youth staff. I did help him clean it up, though.

Mandi: If I did that, I think he'd have a heart attack, fire me, or both.

If you aren't compatible with your senior pastor, get out of there as quickly as possible, or else you will have serious consequences later.

(BURNED OUT, NAZARENE, SUBURBAN TENNESSEE)

| | |
|---|---|
| *Bonnie*: | Maybe my husband can bake a pie for your pastor, too. You know—it can be kind of like ghostwriting. |
| *Mandi*: | I'm okay with making pies myself. |
| *Dave*: | I've been silent through all this, and I think it's because I'm kind of jealous. My pastor is distant and aloof. He's nearly ready to retire, and I guess he was raised in an era that wasn't so open and free. Maybe he thinks all fun is sinful or something, especially in the church. I do compliment him and pray for him. I'm sure he'd be confused, and probably hurt and angry, if I played a joke on him. But I've accepted my situation. The youth group is going well, and he is supportive. |

Time, encouragement, not placing blame on others, being content, good communication, empathetic understanding—these are all important ways to build bridges with the senior pastors and board members at our churches. When we're doing these things, we are building fences that help keep us from failure, making it less likely that we'll burn out and leave or get asked to leave.

Of course, there's more. We've also got to work well with parents—and kids, too. Now let's consider how to work positively with each of those groups.

## CHAPTER 8

# WORKING POSITIVELY WITH PARENTS— AND KIDS

## PARENTS: MOST OF THEM REALLY CARE

"Pastor Len, I can't believe you did this," began Mrs. Carlson.

My adrenaline started to rise. Another in a series of tense exchanges. "You told us parents that Roger was one of the chaperones. I let Sara go on the trip based on the fact there was at least one adult there whom I could trust—not just college kids."

Mentally, I was heading for my bunker. The college visitation weekend had a year's worth of problems packed into a few miserable days. Roger had phoned only two days before the trip to let me know he couldn't go. Though I was not going on the trip either, I still felt confident that we had sufficient staff along, including the youth pastor of another church. The kid/staff ratio met our guidelines.

Mrs. Carlson continued, "When I saw that everything had been changed, I felt like you had lied. You said one thing and did another. I was so angry— you took away any control or option I had as a parent. I almost didn't let Sara get on the bus, but that would have created a big scene in the parking lot."

One of my policies is: *When in doubt, apologize.*

"I understand how surprised and disturbed you must have felt, Mrs. Carlson, when you saw the staffing change. There was nothing I could do about

Roger backing out at the last minute. We had enough adults going to meet our guidelines. I really apologize for..."

"Your apologies mean nothing, Len. Apologies are cheap; you say a few words, then you go on your own merry way. I don't count college kids as staff, and you know that. They don't have near the maturity, and you know that. And when I heard that the bus broke down four times, and they drove with a possibility of brake failure..."

After this conversation, I stared out the window for a long while. Damage control time. "If you can't stand the heat, get out of the kitchen," I reminded myself. "I wonder if Grace Church is still looking for a youth pastor—I hear they pay really well. Hmmm, I wish I were filthy rich and didn't have to work at all. Retiring at age 30 does have its appeal. Or maybe I should just work at Home Depot or Starbucks for the rest of my life..."

> A great way for a youth pastor to avoid getting fired is to make sure expectations are very clearly spelled out in writing *before* accepting the position. The youth pastor should ask the senior pastor if he/she has had difficulties with staff before and how that was handled.
>
> (FIRED, BAPTIST, RURAL CALIFORNIA)

Eventually I was able to pray about my feelings and get back on my feet. I wondered if Mrs. Carlson's tsunami of anger was going to be the worst, or if there were higher waves yet to come. I've learned that parental reactions to youth ministry misfortunes vary from case to case. Sometimes the worst reactions come first. Sometimes the first complaint is only a faint hint of the wrath yet to come. This time none of the other parents were *that* upset. The Carlsons left the church a few months later, as did the chairman of our transportation committee, upon whom parental anger about the church bus was vented.

And so it goes when working with parents. We win some and we lose some. Some will rise up and call us blessed. Others will rise up and call for our execution.

Just as we must seek to work positively with our senior pastor and the board, so it should be with parents. And many of the same skills are required. To have a good working relationship with the parents of our youth, we need to 1) understand them, 2) have integrity ourselves, and 3) build bridges.

## UNDERSTANDING PARENTS

Parenting isn't child's play. It can be hard, frustrating, and unrewarding. Some parents may have extreme anxiety about the safety of their kids day to day. Others may be worrying about whether their kids will be admitted to Ivy League schools. Many parents feel they've completely lost control of their kids, with the rise of the Internet, media downloads, and social networking technology. They fear their kids will make mistakes that will impair them for life.

If we don't pay attention to the fears and anxieties of parents, we are in for big trouble. To ignore parents is to invite misunderstanding and conflict. Yet it's important to realize that parental fear and anxiety about their kids can actually be the thing that puts them on our side. If we work hard to build good relationships with the parents, to understand the hopes and dreams they have for their kids, as well as the fears and concerns, our ministry can soar. Sure it is easier to work successfully with parents when we are forty (and often parents ourselves) than when we are only 19, but it is possible to have a credible ministry with parents, even if we are barely out of high school ourselves. Let's take some time to think about some of the challenges parents face, and how they can affect our ministries.

*Life Cycles and Seasons.* None of the parents in your church have *any* previous experience being their current ages. At ages 35 to 55, parents are experiencing many personal pressures. With changes in our rapidly globalizing economy, many parents feel their jobs are insecure. While the previous generation of parents may have enjoyed a lifetime job with good benefits working for the same company, many parents today face not only job insecurity but reduction of benefits as health care and insurance costs escalate.

Add to the economic pressures the personal pressures of being a single parent or trying to maintain a healthy marriage. Many men and women marry their opposites when it comes to personality. It's all very alluring and attractive at first. After a few years, however, those differences require significant emotional energy to bridge, especially when times are tough.

Another relational issue many parents face (which was likely not faced by their parents) often occurs when both spouses work full time and have children as well. In these two-career families, parents can be so tired and stressed that romantic feelings are very hard to come by, and the marriage can easily become sexless.[1] This produces loneliness and makes one vulnerable to "falling in love" with someone at work who seems "more compatible." If you are in youth ministry any significant length of time, you will likely witness men and women leaving their spouses and children to "find themselves" with other romantic interests.

I remember a conversation with 16-year-old Jenny, who sat in my office, her eyes reddening. "There's something wrong with my dad," she said.

I'm no great counselor, but I was wise enough to say, "That must be really hard on you. Tell me more..." I was expecting her to say her dad had been diagnosed with cancer or something, but it wasn't that at all.

"He's just not with us anymore. I mean, he is at home for supper, that kind of thing, but his mind is not with us. My younger brother is clueless, but I can see my mom starting to panic."

Only three weeks later Jenny's father announced to his wife of 20 years, his 16-year-old daughter, and his 13-year-old son that he had found a true love, and was initiating divorce proceedings so he could marry his soulmate.

The week of her dad's announcement, something occurred to Jenny. Ten months earlier her father had inexplicably decided their family should leave the very small church they'd long attended and begin attending our church, which was very large. The family had switched churches at his insistence. Jenny now realized her father's plan all along was to extricate himself from the sticky web of relationships and accountability in their previous church. As a newcomer at our larger church, he could remain relatively anonymous and wouldn't have to face people who would confront him about his poor choices.

Another pressure many parents face concerns health, or lack of it. The health of their own parents may be failing, which has various financial and personal implications. They may also be facing serious health concerns of their own, particularly with issues stemming from decades of unhealthy eating and continuous weight gain. As the inescapable evidence mounts, parents conclude that their bodies will not last forever—they are mortal.

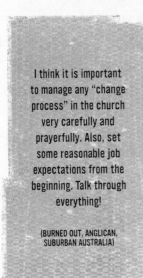

I think it is important to manage any "change process" in the church very carefully and prayerfully. Also, set some reasonable job expectations from the beginning. Talk through everything!

(BURNED OUT, ANGLICAN, SUBURBAN AUSTRALIA)

Add to this gloomy picture a strong-willed teenager or two, and the feeling of life satisfaction in the home can plummet. I lost count long ago of how many parents I've seen grieve over the rebelliousness of their teenagers. The challenges of such parenting can often place great strain on a marriage. What to do about Debbie on drugs or Madison who's pregnant or Conner who's often drunk? Unanimity can come hard for these couples.

Feelings of guilt over lack of time spent with kids can also be a major issue for parents, particularly in two-income marriages. There just aren't enough hours outside the workplace to spend much time at all with their kids—let alone quality time. Parents may feel trapped by this situation—they want to make time with their kids a priority, but they can't cut back on work and still afford the lifestyle the family enjoys.

The upside of all this downside is *parents know they need help.* For this reason, large churches that can afford quality youth programs usually see an influx of Christian families. A small church with no youth group may seem fine to most parents when the children are little. But when Shannon and David start hitting the upper elementary years, their parents start to panic. They want a church that will offer solid ministry for their kids—and for them, too, if possible. What, specifically, do Christian parents want?

The research of Dr. Merton Strommen, founder of the Search Institute, tells us Christian parents want five things:[2]

1. To understand themselves and their kids.

2. To have a close family.

3. To see their kids behave morally.

4. To have a sense of shared faith with their kids.

5. To have access to outside help.

Number five is the primary place where we come in. Our churches have parents who are hurting yet hopeful, and expecting the youth ministry will be a meaningful part of their kids' lives. They want us to be their allies as they parent their kids. They don't expect us to counsel them or tell them how to raise their kids (at least not until we have teenagers of our own), but they want us to have them "on the radar."

Before we can do this, however, we need to act in ways that assure parents that they can trust us. A big part of this trust involves our personal integrity with respect to parents.

> Never cut parents out of the ministry. They must be involved and stay involved. Never take your work home, and take vacations and time off when needed. Have a separate group of friends (not the kids, not the parents) that you stay involved with and who are supportive of you.
>
> (FIRED, UNITED METHODIST, SUBURBAN NEW JERSEY)

## THE YOUTH WORKER'S PERSONAL INTEGRITY AND PARENTS

Until we have teenage children of our own, we may find it difficult to understand and appreciate the parents' point of view—and this is especially true for youth pastors under age twenty-five. One sign of personal integrity and maturity in ministry is consciously considering the parental perspective on our decisions.

> We fired our youth pastor because he only acted
> like a big kid. There was no separation between
> how the kids acted and how he did. This guy was
> like a 16-year-old and soon both the kids and the
> parents wanted him out.

There are many positive, practical ways we can demonstrate to parents that we understand their point of view. Sharing their concern for *safety* is a big one.

I was 19—and pretty much totally oblivious to parental concerns about safety—when I was hired by a church to be their junior high youth director. At the time I was deeply in love with my new Camaro. One Friday evening I packed 11 junior high kids (no kidding) into that car and went cruising. Have you ever seen how small a Camaro is on the inside? There were five of us in the front (including one straddling the stick shift) and seven in the back. The kids thought I was a god. I (apparently) thought I was a god. The patrolman who pulled me over thought somewhat less of me and my actions. The parents who eventually heard about this incident wrote me off as immature and even dangerous.

It may not come naturally, but we *must* think about safety if we hope to have integrity as youth pastors. Youth workers who want to drive church vehicles like fighter pilots or Halo 2-vintage banshees need not apply. I have all my youth ministry students read Jack Crabtree's book *Better Safe than Sued*, and it scares them to death. And that's good. It helps them see that parents expect their kids will come home from youth group meetings and events with all their body parts intact. It helps them see that, when it comes to retreats, bringing back 95 percent of the kids is not good enough.

The parents' point of view also involves *the clock*. We have integrity when we end our youth meetings and events when we say they'll end. Sure, running a little overtime every once in a while is not a big problem, but make it a pattern, and your stock will go down.

The middle school group with which I volunteer meets in a house owned by the church. Kids usually start arriving around 7:00 p.m. and usually play games or just hang out until we begin, officially, at 7:30. Our meetings run until 9:00. New Yorkers are very time conscious, and many parents are waiting in their cars outside by 8:55. If the meeting goes past 9:05, some will come into the entrance hallway, just around the corner from our meeting room. If it gets to be 9:10, they will, without hesitation, come into the meeting room and motion for their kids to come out. This may sound pretty uptight, but it was no different in the other places I served as youth pastor—Vancouver, BC; New Jersey; and even laid-back Seattle. Woe be it to any youth leader who habitually fails at clock management when it comes to youth group meetings. If we continually frustrate parents about issues related to time, we make it harder for them to feel we care about them or their (busy) lives.

Parents also need to know *whose side we are on*, when it comes to their kids. As youth pastors, we may hear kids say a lot of negative things about their parents. That is not surprising. But if we always join in and speak about parents as the bad guys, we lack integrity. We may not want to admit it, but most parents are right most of the time when it comes to their kids. They know them better than we do, they love them more than we do, and their relationships with their children will continue long after we have left the scene. Yes, parents sometimes do and say unbelievably stupid things to their teenagers, but they are not always wrong. We have integrity if we seek to partner with them in ministry to their teenagers.

Some youth workers have trouble getting along with parents because they have trouble getting along with adults in general. Much of this interaction will be determined by *how well we got along with our own parents*.

Way back in the 1980s I was struck by the wisdom in an article by Paul Thigpen, who told the story of a youth worker named Josh.[3] In the years since then, I've met plenty of "Joshes." Thigpen writes:

His complaints were always the same: The pastor and the church were rigid and old fashioned. They never allowed him the freedom to make his own decisions. Though the kids loved him, their parents did not respect him. Everyone was critical of him, he said...even his wife.

During one of his complaining sessions, I decided to ask Josh a few questions about his parents. Josh's turbulent adolescence had been a rebellion against a tyrannical father and a critical mother. After college he had moved across the country to escape them, but somehow they seemed to have come along in his emotional baggage. His wife had begun to remind him of his mother, and the senior pastor was "just like" his father...He found himself resenting any kind of authority, reacting fiercely to criticism, and feeling more like one of the kids than one of the adults.

Is baggage about your own parents dragging down your ministry? Thigpen's questionnaire can help you think about this. Put a check by each statement that is generally true for you:

## In My Youth Ministry

____ I automatically side with kids in my group who are in conflict with parents.

____ I frequently feel resentment toward the parents of my youth group kids.

____ I criticize parents when talking with kids.

____ I have frequent conflicts with those in authority over me— senior pastor, church board, church council, or board of deacons.

___ I tend to look to senior staff members as parent figures and feel frustrated when they do not meet my emotional needs.

___ I look to kids to give me a sense of acceptance and approval.

___ I frequently feel left out, unappreciated, or taken for granted by other staff members.

## In My Personal Life

___ I see the same problems emerging in my marriage (or romantic relationships) that I had with my parent of the opposite sex.

___ I have a persistent struggle with anger.

___ I find myself treating my own children in ways I disliked being treated as a child.

___ I dread having to call, e-mail, or visit my parents.

___ I regress to a childhood or adolescent role when I visit my parents.

___ I still compare myself to my siblings.

___ I frequently feel disappointed or bitter about work, family, relationships, God, or life in general.

If you find that you checked many of the items above, you've got parental baggage that is likely to affect your integrity with the parents in your student ministry. Some time with a good counselor may help you with these issues, but Thigpen suggests the following as a place to begin:

1. Make a list of your parents' offenses against you.

2. Remember your offenses against them.

3.  Find someone to listen to all this.

4.  Seek to understand your parents.

5.  Forgive your parents, and yourself.

6.  Begin to assume responsibility for your life.

When you try to understand parents and decide to make personal integrity with parents a high priority, you create a good foundation to build on with the parents of your youth group kids.

## BUILDING BRIDGES WITH PARENTS

There are many roles we can play in relationship to parents, even if we ourselves are barely out of adolescence. For parents, we serve as a resource person, a facilitator of other resources, a friend, and an encourager. Here are some practical steps we can take to build bridges with the parents of our youth:

*Acting Like an Adult.* If we're working in church-based youth ministry, it's likely that parents may invite us to their homes for a meal. Parents want to get to know us; they want to support us. It's important to know what constitutes "adult behavior" in this social setting. I teach my youth ministry students that adult behavior in the "home for a meal" scenario generally includes these features: 1) When invited, immediately ask what you can bring (such as rolls or a salad or dessert). If the answer is "nothing," be sure to bring a small gift, like flowers, nuts, or candy. 2) Arrive within 10 minutes of the stated time, having turned your cell phone off. 3) Around the table, always remember to pass the food to the next person when it comes in your direction and be sure to engage any children present in conversation along with the teenagers and adults. 4) Finally, if you're invited to bring your boyfriend/girlfriend or spouse, don't be hanging all over each other as if you're about to have sex in the car the moment you leave.

I don't know if this list of "dinner rules" is exactly right all over the world, but I know it applies in Manila, Singapore, London,

Belfast, Amsterdam, the Canadian Provinces of British Columbia and Saskatchewan, and most of the United States. If you have any doubt about what behavior is expected in your context, ask someone you trust to fill you in. If you're a young youth pastor who gets this right, chances are the parents will be impressed by your maturity and will tell their friends what an excellent youth worker you are. The goal isn't to score points with parents. But we must recognize that, if parents have high regard for us, our ministry possibilities will expand and we will likely feel supported and respected. All of these things help serve as burnout or "fire" prevention.

*Newsletters*, sent out monthly or (at least) quarterly, will let parents know that we want to be in touch. Newsletters can talk about upcoming events, ask for prayer, and present helpful material about youth, parenting, and youth culture that we've gleaned from our other reading.

*Parent Seminars* can build bridges as well. Good resources are available on DVD, and there might be counselors or other resource people in our own or nearby congregations who could make presentations. I love to do parent panels—particularly with parents of middle school kids—asking them to address issues like cell phones, social networking sites on the Internet, "in" hours, television time, and other concerns they confront as parents.

*Parent Support Groups* and/or *Parent Prayer Groups* can be tremendously important. Those parents whose young people are in complete rebellion are often especially hungry for the peer support that such groups can provide.

*Parent Meetings* can serve as a valuable venue to conveying information and getting feedback. Even brief gatherings immediately after the Sunday worship service can be very important in helping parents feel valued and informed. A word to the wise: Whenever you have a parent meeting, write up a summary and mail it to all parents—including those who weren't there. You can't force every parent to read it, but no one can say you didn't try to communicate.

I can't guarantee that parents will hoist you to their shoulders and sing "hosanna" while carrying you around the church because you followed these steps. But I do believe your organized efforts here will build bridges. Get out your calendar, lay out your plan (meetings, seminars, resources, etc.), print up a one-year schedule on quality paper, and give copies to all the parents as well as all members of the church board. As you go through the year, recruit some key parents to work with you to determine the coming year's "parent ministry" plan.

When parents see that you care about them as well as their kids, they'll be more likely to give you more latitude to try new things. Were it not for the good foundation I'd established with parents, I could never have taken kids Christmas caroling on porno row in downtown Seattle, or had a non-Christian philosophy professor come and share with our high school Sunday school class why she'd chosen *not* to be a Christian.

That same foundation of trust and understanding can be especially important when things go wrong. I remember a time when I took the youth from my Seattle church on a weekend ski retreat. The first part of the retreat had gone great. We'd slept on the floor of a church near Whistler Mountain, British Columbia, on Friday night, skied all day Saturday, and were excited about spending the rest of the weekend in the beautiful city of Vancouver. A month earlier, I'd reserved rooms for us at a place I'd found in the city visitor's guide. City Motel was to be our headquarters for the night.

Thinking back on it later, the sign behind the registration desk did strike me as a little odd: "NO ILLEGAL ACTIVITIES ALLOWED ON THE PREMISES." But I didn't give it much thought. After confirming that the motel had received our full payment in the mail a month earlier, I walked back out to help the senior highers unload the church bus.

A police car roared in from Main Street and stopped a yard from me. The officer got out and approached me. Looking like he was confused, or lost, or something, he asked me: "What are you doing?"

"Well, officer," I replied, "As you see here, we're unloading the church bus. We're from Seattle, we were at Whistler today, and now we're going to stay here."

"Don't you know what this is?"

My life began to pass before my eyes. "What do you mean?"

"This is a house of prostitution that serves this end of the city. Better keep a close watch on your kids."

"Thanks..." My voice trailed off as he returned to his patrol car.

My mind was a blur. We had no money, there was no place else to stay, and most of the kids had heard this conversation. No wonder the rates at City Motel were so cheap. I could already imagine the newspaper headlines when this story got out: "Youth Pastor Jailed for Own Protection as Angry Parents Picket Church."

Fortunately, our bus driver was a respected church elder. I called him aside. With a gleam in his eye, he said, "I think God wants us to take this place over." That's all I needed to hear— because I was starting to think the same thing.

We moved into our rooms. They were so dirty that most of us went right back to the bus to get our sleeping bags. The hotel towels were paper-thin and stained. I crammed everyone into my room, and we discussed our situation. Then we held a wonderful (and loud) time of worship and prayer right there.

Just as the officer predicted, it was a very busy night. Male and female customers came and went all night. Most of us didn't sleep very well. We were glad to get out the door and on to Grouse Mountain for more skiing the next day before heading home. As far as I know, I'm the only youth pastor in history to have a retreat in a bordello.

When we got back, the church elder who'd driven the bus took the initiative to call key parents and explain what happened. His support was critical. But I think a mistake that spectacular was forgivable only because the parents knew that I cared about them and their concerns as parents. I had earned their trust.

Understanding, having integrity, and building bridges with parents: They work together only to not further our ministries, but reduce criticism. We're building fences against failure and burnout when we do these things.

And what about kids? Of course books galore are written about working with kids, and I'll have more to say about the particular challenges of building bridges with both churched and unchurched kids in chapter 10. But first let's take a quick look at how these same issues of understanding and integrity apply in our direct work with youth.

# WORKING WITH KIDS: TWO KEY IDEAS TO HELP YOU SLEEP BETTER AT NIGHT—AND KEEP YOU OUT OF PRISON

## Understanding the Teenage Mind

In order to work positively with young people, we have to understand how they think. We also need to have a sense of what constitutes normal kid behavior.

Relax, I'm not going to rehearse long passages from Piaget, Fowler, Kohlberg, and other luminaries in the academic study of adolescent development. There is one important idea, however, that every youth pastor had better get a grip on. If you don't, you'll find your stomach is often upset in youth ministry...and it won't be the food that causes it. Until I understood it, I lost sleep because I couldn't figure out what was wrong—and I've known many other youth workers who were on the fast track to burnout until they began to understand the implications of what I call *the cerebral upgrade.*

## Take this simple five-question quiz:

1.  The reason many 12-to-15-year-old boys are spiritual nerds compared to many 12-to-15-year-old girls is:

    ___ a.  God is female and she relates better to girls.

    ___ b.  Girls imitate the spirituality of more mature people, but boys don't.

    ___ c.  Girls gain the ability to think abstractly before boys.

2. Young people's decisions to commit or recommit their lives to Christ will be more likely to last when:

___ a.   It snows in Hawaii.

___ b.   The youth worker is physically attractive.

___ c.   They are juniors or seniors in high school.

3. Much of church is boring to middle school/junior high kids because:

___ a.   They want to get home and do their homework.

___ b.   The pastor is not a sports megahero.

___ c.   The prayers and sermons are too long and not in their language.

4. Young people can have a truly biblically based self-esteem when:

___ a.   They obtain their own copy of the NIV Student Study Bible.

___ b.   They are better looking than most others in the youth group.

___ c.   They are mature enough to think about the fact that they are thinking (that is, they can think abstractly).

5. When a kid in my youth group questions the existence of God, I should:

___ a.   Call the elders/deacons/pastor.

___ b.   Pray that he/she will be healed of doubt.

___ c.   Thank God because the kid is right on schedule.

If you haven't guessed already, the correct answer to each of the questions above is "c." These answers tell us a bit about the amazing things that happen in the brains of young people during adolescence. During the teenage years, new mental wires are continually getting made and connected. Previously unused brain capacity is aroused into life. The mind of a child changes, often within a period of only a few months, into an entirely different organ. This cerebral upgrade starts occurring in girls first, usually between the ages of 11 and 14. Most boys, for reasons known only to God, don't get the upgrade until age 15 or later.

The prefrontal cortex is the area of the brain from which risk assessment, ability to think and make plans about the future, and abstract thinking arises. Early adolescent boys may have a prefrontal cortex, but it is not plugged in yet. The lights may be on, but no one is home. The prefrontal cortex of most girls is functioning by age 12. Most boys still don't have this level of thinking even by age 14.

Youth who have experienced this upgrade in brain development can make faith more than just a hand-me-down from their parents. They can *reason* and understand why Jesus died for them. They can understand and embrace the gospel at a whole new level that was not previously possible. The process may be messy with questions: *Why should I believe in God? Isn't Islam just as good as or better than Christianity? How can something that happened so long ago make a difference today?* If our youth are asking these questions, that's a good sign!

When it comes to self-esteem, the average seventh–grade boy won't feel secure unless he has the material things or abilities his peers admire. But in a few years, he'll be able to understand who he is in Christ and the true foundation and comfort this brings.

When we understand these facts of adolescent brain development, we don't spend so many sleepless nights wondering why the junior high boys don't "get it." We can take comfort in knowing that most of them will, in time. When it comes to kid behavior, understanding the cerebral upgrade can also make us a bit more sympathetic toward young male acting-out. The part of their brains that sees themselves and assesses risk is, quite literally, not plugged in yet. Of course, we youth workers must be clear about behavioral expectations and provide clear and meaningful consequences for noncooperation (such as a time-out if a boy doesn't settle down when appropriate).

# SEXUAL INTEGRITY AROUND KIDS

Have sex with a kid in your youth group, and you'll likely go to prison. By "having sex" I don't just mean having intercourse. Laws regarding "statutory rape" also forbid other sexual touching between adults and minors. In chapter 2 I gave a few examples of cases where lives and ministries were destroyed by sexual impropriety. Unfortunately, I could have filled a whole book with the stories of lives damaged by sexual activity between youth workers and youth. Here, let me offer you a few guidelines—drawn from personal experience, observation, and academic study—to help you safeguard your ministry and avoid such tragic mistakes.

First, recognize that you (yes, *you*) are capable of spectacular moral failure when it comes to young people. I know some who read this won't believe you could ever make such a terrible mistake, but both male and female youth workers can stumble here. Even though it may be hard to believe, you must admit you are human and capable of error. Realize the truth of 1 Peter 5:8: "Your enemy the devil prowls around like a roaring lion looking for someone to devour." We're talking here about *your* enemy, and the person he wants to devour is *you.*

> Communicate more than you think is necessary with all stakeholders, most notably the parents. Let the parents know what the plans are and solicit input and active (not passive) help.
>
> (FIRED, BAPTIST, SUBURBAN FLORIDA)

Second, recognize what kinds of situations and circumstances leave you most vulnerable to inappropriate sexual interest. Is it when you are mad at your spouse and surrounded by adoring adolescents? Is it when you've had a series of high-intensity ministry days and you're just tired and needing some comfort or relief? Is it when you're on a summer retreat and have spent the day romping in the lake with scantily clad girls or guys with "nice butts" and you find yourself wondering if a certain kid needs your extra attention? Is it when you feel misunderstood and you just want someone to hug and comfort you—and into your mind pops a certain kid who's pretty good at hugs? Know yourself and when you are most vulnerable, and take special precautions at these times.

Third, set up, with other volunteers or staff people, solid rules to protect yourself. Don't put yourself in situations where you are alone with a youth of the opposite sex, including car rides. Side hugs only—not frontal. No wrestling with kids of the opposite sex, even in the snow.

Fourth, don't go another week without *real accountability*. Have at least one person with whom you meet, either face-to-face or online, who will regularly ask you the hard questions you might want to ignore. Questions like: Are you thinking about any particular kid(s) in ways that are sexual? Are you trying to touch or sit next to a particular kid more than any other? Do you find the attention of a particular kid of special interest or meaning to you? If you are married, your accountability partner should ask you about your sex life. Is your sex life good? If not, what can you do to have real romance in your marriage? If you're single, have your accountability partner ask about your online wanderings, or about any magazines hidden away from view, or what you think about when the lights go off at night.

Finally, don't forget what Jesus did when he faced temptation. Remember when Jesus faced those three temptations in the wilderness (Matthew 4)? How did he respond to each one? He quoted Scripture. Here are two of my favorite passages to use when faced with temptation:

> In the same way, count yourselves dead to sin, but alive to God in Christ Jesus. (Romans 6:11)

> Blessed are the pure in heart, for they will see God. (Matthew 5:8)

THE YOUTH MINISTRY SURVIVAL GUIDE: HOW TO THRIVE AND LAST FOR THE LONG HAUL

We've taken a long look at sources of potential conflict in youth ministry: pastors, church leaders, parents, and even the youth themselves. We've seen some positive steps that can take us away from being fired or burning out ourselves and move us toward a ministry that is flourishing. Now, let's look at a special topic that was virtually absent in my research 15 years ago, but is a big deal today.

# CHAPTER 9

# REACHING THE LOST WITHOUT FRUSTRATING THE FOUND

Is it possible to build a church-based youth program that ministers effectively to kids within the church while still reaching out to youth in the wider community? I believe the answer is yes—but clearly this is a key question for many youth workers. Our survey included dozens of fired or burned-out youth workers who talked about their extreme frustration as they built ministries that were effective in reaching unchurched kids—and then found their own churches standing against them in this effort. Here's how a respondent described the church conflict that led to one youth pastor's dismissal:

> Our church is in a rural setting, and we were glad to have a youth pastor. It didn't take long, though, before it was pretty clear his mind and heart were for "troubled" kids rather than church kids. He wasn't a great teacher, and some of our own church kids started to go to a different youth group in town where they felt more welcome and liked the atmosphere better. They didn't like the rowdy factor the new kids brought to our group. Finally, it all got to be too much, and the church leaders told the youth pastor to leave.

Here, we're at the heart of real struggle and stress for some youth workers. Over 30 percent of the fired youth workers in our survey listed "philosophy of ministry" as one of the primary issues, and most of those elaborated with stories like the one above. Consider the similar themes in these other statements from the survey:

> There was no public outreach for youth allowed.

> Some elders and parents were upset about the "skater kids" who were coming to group.

> Key parents wanted an event-driven ministry geared toward "church kids only."

> One adult leader and some parents did not want there to be a constant influx of new teenagers into the youth ministry.

> Bret was running an aggressive youth outreach program. In his final year in ministry, 85 high school kids came to Christ and were baptized. The church was not ready for this kind of growth—costs, use of building, and so on. The church was made up of largely older people who had a hard time with these other unchurched kids. This growth led to conflicts with the parents ("Why is my kid left out?" "more Bible study needed," "I don't want my kid around these new ones."). The parents got to the board, and Bret was told he was fired. He had been there four years.

Even if they aren't fired, youth pastors who find themselves in this situation of "church kids vs. unchurched kids" can easily feel inadequate, lose confidence, and face constant criticism. Those in the survey who left because of burnout often named these three factors (23 percent, 26 percent, and 36 percent, respectively).

Some of us might find it impossible to believe that any parents or church leaders would be against outreach. But our survey amply shows it is quite possible. Church people have the nerve to believe the youth pastor will have some kind of significant ministry among church kids. Sure, they want us (at least in theory) to reach the world for Christ, but many of them would prefer that we focus primarily on "reaching the reached." And when our ministries do extend to the unreached kids in the community, church people may prefer that the "formerly lost" not get too mixed in with the long-time-found.

Those of us who feel a deep burden to reach lost kids may be tempted to pronounce judgment on any congregation that doesn't share our vision and passion. But let's hold off on the prophetic judgment for a while and try to understand what's going on.

## INSIDE OUT VS. OUTSIDE IN

Many youth workers have an "aha" moment when they hear about the insights of Pete Ward at the University of London/Kings College. Consider these two diagrams, which refer to the *role of the youth worker.*

### INSIDE-OUT

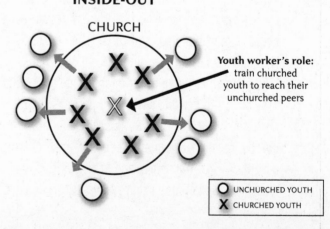

CHURCH

Youth worker's role:
train churched youth to reach their unchurched peers

○ UNCHURCHED YOUTH
X CHURCHED YOUTH

The role of the youth worker in the Inside Out approach is to work with, nurture, and equip the churched kids to reach out themselves to their non-Christian friends. In this approach, a healthy ratio might be one in which about 80 percent of the youth attending a student ministry regularly are churched kids with the remaining 20 percent being their nonchurched friends who have become believers recently or are in the process of becoming believers. The Inside Out approach is the way most churches see youth ministry. This encompasses the "Purpose Driven" and Sonlife ministry models, as well as most any other ministry model that has a funnel diagram that begins with unchurched youth at the top and disciples coming out at the bottom.

Occasionally I meet a youth pastor who clearly has no heart for Christian kids in the church. They tend to see these kids as spoiled complainers. Such youth workers are much better suited for a parachurch model of ministry, which is otherwise known as "Outside In":

**OUTSIDE-IN**

CHURCH OR FORMING CHRISTIAN GROUP

**Youth worker's role:** go directly to non-Christian youth and win them and bring them into church or newly forming Christian group

O NON-CHRISTIAN YOUTH
X CHURCHED YOUTH

The role of youth workers in the Outside In approach is to go directly to the nonchurched kids, seek to win them to Christ, and then invite them into the church youth group or some other venue for Christian growth. This is the essence of the parachurch model for youth ministry. It's the model used by Young Life, Youth for Christ, and a host of other ministries founded by men and women so passionate about winning the lost they don't want the burden of

GOOD NEWS: THERE'S A TEENAGER IN YOUR LIFE!

seeking approval from church boards, committees, or well-meaning church parents who ultimately want only what's best for their own kids.

Understanding these different concepts of ministry can be very helpful. Some of my students see this and know instantly that they are called to parachurch ministry. When these students graduate, outreach groups like Youth for Christ, Young Life, and various Christian camps and other organizations welcome them with open arms. (I do warn them that one downside to the parachurch model is that they may spend a lot of time raising their own financial support.)

Sometimes I'll meet a youth pastor who's been hired by a church that has no kids within its current congregation. The church has realized this problem and often gives such pastors complete freedom to go to the streets directly and win 'em, win 'em, and win 'em some more. One such youth pastor I met recently is Cairn from Dundee, Scotland. Her church is comprised almost entirely of senior citizens who suddenly realized the church was 10 years from extinction. In her two years at the church, Cairn has seen 20 street kids come to Christ and get involved in the student cell groups she has started. Once a month she has "cell group Sunday" where these kids also come to the church service. The rector lets them read Scripture or pray, and they often perform a worship song (think hip-hop or heavy metal) that expresses their passion for Jesus. Amazingly, the older people in this church have made room for this almost-from-a-different-planet expression of the Christian faith from these street kids.

## NEW KIDS=GROWTH, GROWTH=CHANGE, CHANGE=LOSS

It's good to remember that some people just don't like change—of any sort. Some Golden Retrievers and Ants (see Chapter 5) tend to be especially uncomfortable with change—even a positive change like having new kids coming to youth group. What groups within the church might feel a loss if a youth group grows as unchurched kids begin attending?

*The kids in the youth group* may feel like they've lost the comfort of a close-knit group of friends where everyone feels good about everyone else. Their schools can be confusing and stress-producing, but in youth group they've always known who and what to expect. The big-fish-in-a-small-pond leaders may lose their official or unofficial leadership roles in the group.

The *adult volunteers* may lose the comfort of knowing and being known by every kid, and knowing what to expect. Volunteers may often come to youth group with their minds full of the problems and concerns of the day just finished. Their work lives provide all the change, stress, and challenge they can handle. They help at youth group because they love kids and know involvement in ministry is (or should be) part of a normal Christian life. But a growing youth ministry may threaten the level of comfort they feel.

*Parents* of churched kids aren't always wild about having new kids enter the group either. Parents tend to choose a church they believe will meet the needs of their own kids. A growing youth group may dilute the level of personal care their children receive. Parent may also be concerned that unchurched youth new to the group will be a "bad influence" on their own kids.

> Understand the values of the church. Don't try to change everything at once in the ministry, take on small changes first.
>
> (FIRED, NONDENOMINATIONAL, URBAN INDIA)

The *church board* may be uncomfortable with an influx of new kids because of "wear and tear" on the church building, pressure on the church budget for increases in youth ministry funding, and requests for big-ticket expenses like vans or mission trips. There may be complaints about cigarette butts in the parking lot or items gone missing from the kitchen.

But these concerns don't have to stand in the way of a growing youth program. Most kids, parents, and church boards will welcome new youth if the youth leader is mindful of the possible pitfalls of youth ministry numerical growth. There are several remedies to the aversion to growth we have been talking about.

## Remedy 1: Understand the Impact of Change

If we understand the dynamics of change, we are better able to speak to the concerns of those who fear growth. Dr. Robert Anderson of Western Baptist Seminary reminds us of seven reasons people resist change:[1]

- Change is uncomfortable for them.

- They are not convinced change is necessary.

- They lack confidence in their leaders.

- They do not "own" the change.

- They are uncertain where change will lead.

- They are tired of continuous change.

- They are afraid of losing something.


It isn't hard to see how these reasons might apply to some youth, parents, staff, or board members, particularly those who have Golden Retriever or Ant attributes.

However, Anderson also points out that people will change—and even change happily—when other things are true.

- They are convinced change is legitimate.

- They see the old system as no longer meeting needs.

- They know they no longer have the answers.

- Their attitudes have been changed.


When we understand the reasons people are resistant to change, we can see why it may not be best to show up at our first parents meeting and boldly announce that it's our goal to see the youth group double in the next four weeks. Instead, we should proceed with wise caution, recognizing the fears some may have and helping them move beyond their reservations.

## Remedy 2: Reaching the Reached before Reaching the Unreached

It's true. Most church people have the nerve to believe that our job, whether we are volunteers or paid staff members, is first to reach the church kids. They expect we'll follow the classic "Inside Out" model, believing that if we lay a solid foundation among the youth within the church already, then outreach and numerical growth will follow as a natural result. This imitates the ministry model of Christ, who poured himself into his disciples before sending them out to reach others.

I appreciate the approach of Sonlife, a parachurch ministry that serves the church by helping youth workers (first) model their lives after that of Jesus and then (second) develop youth ministries that reflect the characteristics of those closest to Jesus and the early church. Sonlife contends that ministry in the way of Jesus is founded on a commitment to share life with others through genuine relationships. With this commitment at the foundation, outreach and numerical growth will naturally follow, especially if the youth ministry is also passionate about and committed to the following "inside out" practices of the early church:

- **Teaching the Word:** Helping students know how to feed themselves spiritually

- **Worship and prayer:** Honoring God through our lives and actions

- **Servant actions:** Taking the time to care for others in tangible ways

- **Authentic community:** Providing an encouraging and affirming place for students and volunteers to belong and believe

Sonlife cautions that moving prematurely into outreach without fully establishing a good foundation of living out the virtues of

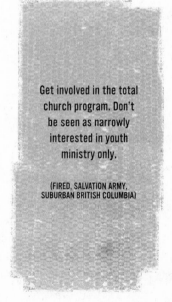

Get involved in the total church program. Don't be seen as narrowly interested in youth ministry only.

(FIRED, SALVATION ARMY, SUBURBAN BRITISH COLUMBIA)

Jesus and modeling after the early church could mean frustration and failure down the line.[2]

## Remedy 3: Create a Ministry That is Geared for Care

Anxiety on the part of students, parents, and staff is greatly reduced if it is obvious that our ministry is structured to promote care and shepherding. The following short quiz will test your insight into this important principle.

Question: One of the best ways to structure a youth ministry for care and meeting of needs is...

_____ a. through small groups

_____ b. through small groups

_____ c. through small groups

_____ d. all of the above

Very good! I've seen volunteers and paid youth workers burn out or get fired because they couldn't figure this out.

Take Carlos, for example. Carlos was the ultimate up-front personality, an excellent speaker, and a dynamic kids-flock-to-him youth worker. And flock to him those kids did! Unfortunately for Carlos and his volunteer staff, he was unable to gear his group for care. Kids were attracted to him and his charisma, but Carlos was always too busy to help them with their personal problems. His staff was like a revolving door; they were recruited to "help" with the youth ministry, but all they did was come and watch him do his thing. Most adults found it very intimidating to come to a group with over 100 kids and just "hang out" or "try to build relationships"!

Eventually, it all fell apart. Carlos couldn't handle the nuts-and-bolts administration of a large group, kids got disillusioned, and other staff members quit in frustration. I have seen many groups follow this same pattern—spectacular growth followed by collapse.

There are many ways a ministry can be structured for care successfully. The junior high group with which I volunteer spends about ten minutes each Wednesday night in small groups. Adult leaders meet with the same group each week. Every kid knows who his or her leader is. All the parents know which leader is meeting with their particular son or daughter. The leaders try to phone or e-mail the kids in their small group during the week to see how they are doing and to let them know they're missed if they are absent.

I was the youth pastor of a church in Seattle for 14 years. The youth group grew to 250 kids—100 junior high and 150 senior high—using the classic "inside out" model. Even with such a large group, we rarely had complaints about kids not being cared for. It was obvious to both kids and parents that each student was part of a 20-30 member "team" that was shepherded by three adult volunteers and three student leaders. Kids felt cared for. These teams met each Wednesday as part of our midweek youth gathering, and within these smaller groups birthdays were acknowledged, newcomers were introduced, and team-specific gatherings were planned. We didn't ask our adult leaders to care for hundreds of kids in a huge group, just the ones in their team. Staff and volunteers felt useful. They didn't come to watch me do my thing; they came to connect with and care for their youth group within the youth group. Most weeks each team broke down into smaller groups of 10 or less, each led by one adult and one student leader. If a team grew larger than 35 youth, we split the group in two and recruited more leaders to help out.

With a team structure like this, there is no limit to how large a group can grow while still making a priority of offering personal care to each kid. Teams or small groups can potentially meet on Sunday mornings as part of Sunday school, as part of a midweek meeting, or off the church property during the week. The concept can be sliced, diced, and served up in a variety of ways, but some kind of small group structure assures kids, staff, and parents that personal care is happening. It gives staff members a very specific and tangible way to serve.

Of course, a team or small group structure means that kids will sometimes come to other adults when they have a problem or crisis, rather than to *you*, the all-powerful youth leader. This is as it should be as a group grows, but it can be a tremendous issue for some youth leaders to put aside their pride and realize kids are better off if personal care is decentralized and not completely dependent on the youth pastor or primary youth leader. Just last week I had breakfast with a youth pastor who told me this has been the single most difficult thing for him personally. As his ministry grew numerically and he started small groups, he found that "most of the kids no longer came to me first." (This same hurdle can also trip up some senior pastors, who may feel very threatened if people in the church don't come to them first in a crisis.),

## Remedy 4: Teach and Train with a Vision for Outreach and Practical Outreach Opportunities

It doesn't require a seminary degree to see that the Bible is full of stories that declare God's passion for outreach. God wants the world to know and experience his love. As we unpack this message among our staff, students, and parents, the question becomes obvious: "So what are we going to do about it?" It helps tremendously if the whole church is being challenged to reach the unreached. But even if this is not the case, we can help our youth reach out to others once we've firmly established an emphasis on feeding and caring for them.

When teenagers begin growing in their Christian lives and understand that the benefits of this life go way beyond "fire insurance," their desire to have friends experience the Good News follows naturally. In our youth group we remind the kids they have been "found" and that God's heart is to reach others through them (again, the classic "inside out" approach). We encourage them to have a "most wanted" list of friends they hope to see come to Christ.

Sometimes I meet a Christian teenager—most often home-schooled or from a Christian school—who does not have a single non-Christian friend to think of or pray for. Usually, this is by in-tentional, protective, parental design. Though I am tempted to pronounce a "thus saith the Lord" judgment on such an approach to parenting, I'm generally able to bite my tongue. I remind these young people that, even if they don't know anyone they can in-vite to become part of the group, they can pray for the friends of others, and be welcoming to newcomers when they actually show up at youth group. I find it helpful to have a personal conversa-tion with homeschool/Christian school parents about this "most wanted" emphasis. I have rarely met any significant resistance to this approach when those parents can clearly see their own kids' needs are being met and they can see how this "most wanted" emphasis connects to the bib-lical call to share the Good News.

When we have a special outreach event, the core kids in our youth group are remind-ed to invite their friends and pray they will come. We commit to be welcoming to all those who do. When the student leadership core group plans an outreach event, we ask the hard question: "So, are you going to invite a friend to this? If the answer is no, we've got to go back to the drawing board."

When the churched youth have been nurtured and geared for outreach, there are several ways to proceed. One approach I love is a low-key "in house" outreach event. This is held once every month or two, on the group's normal meeting night. I plan these nights with the student leadership team (not adults). The newsletter lets parents know about it so they can be praying, and kids are reminded, "Next week, be sure to invite a friend to youth group."

A typical "in house" event is entirely student-led. That is, from start to finish, no adult is standing in front of the group—*ever*.

> There should be classes taught in college on dealing with adversity in Youth Ministry for YM majors! So many students come out of college and, when the first bad thing or conflict comes along, they realize this is not what they signed up for. Interning is great, but you typically don't deal with the irate parent or the elder who doesn't agree with the direction you are heading.
>
> (BURNED OUT, NONDENOMINATIONAL, URBAN MASSACHUSETTS)

This can be very important, not only for those youth attending for the first time, but also for the students taking leadership roles. I once did a study of 500 youth ministries, looking at the factors associated with numerical growth. The number one thing associated with numerical growth over a two-year period was *an increase in the percentage of time kids themselves were standing up front leading the youth group.* (More on this in chapter 10.)

Every outreach event has a theme. It could be "friendship," "disappointment," "being a hero," "revenge," or any other topic the student leaders decide is relevant. The event proceeds in four steps. First, there are a couple of opening mixer-type games that have something, even indirectly, to do with the theme. Next, there is some kind of media presentation—a movie clip, a video game clip, a skit, a song, or some combination of these—that relates directly to the theme. The third stage is a series of three short talks by students, reflecting on how Christ has made a difference to them in relation to the theme. The third kid closes his or her talk by saying something like this:

> "If you're sitting here and you realize we're talking like Jesus is our actual friend and he shows up and does stuff in our lives, maybe you've never heard something like this before and you'd like to find out more. If so, that's great. We're going to pass out the "Name Grabbers" for the drawing now. When you get yours, fill it out like everyone else but put a big "X" on the front. There will be food available right after the Name Grabber drawing, and during that time we can hang out and talk some more about this."

In the youth ministries I've led, we use "Name Grabbers" to keep track of attendance. Everyone fills out the Name Grabber card each week (name on front and, if the kid is new, a little more info on the back). After the cards are collected, there is a drawing for some kind of prize. (On outreach night we try to make sure it's a good prize—like a gift certificate at the favorite pizza place or something.) Once the drawing is held, the prize awarded, and everyone is unleashed on the refreshments, the three student speakers look through the pile of Name Grabbers. Any "Xed" ones are pulled out, and one of the speakers will grab another student leader and go speak with the kid who put the X: "Hey, I see you Xed the Name Grabber. Cool! Let's get our food and go hang out."

One reason this approach to outreach rarely draws criticism from kids or parents is that it is clearly owned entirely by the youth themselves. Even kids who may have no unchurched friends can be involved in presenting the media or giving a talk. If you're looking for a mass evangelism tool, this isn't the method for you—but it can result in a slow infusion of new believers into your youth ministry.

Another benefit is what happens to our churched kids when they actually lead their peers to Christ, as opposed to having the "professional" youth pastor or adult leaders do it. Obviously, this requires training for student leaders—but the training and prayer infrastructure required before something like this is undertaken also builds student ownership.

## OPENING THE DOORS WIDER

Remember that one of the most important things you can do to pave the way for outreach to lost youth is to help your "already found" youth feel cared for and empowered. We'll talk more about empowerment in chapter 10. Before we get there, however, here are a few more practical ideas that may help kids, parents, staff, and boards be more open to newcomers.

Many denominations have major annual or biannual youth conferences. These mega-events often include worship, speakers, and seminars that challenge youth and adult volunteers to live out their faith. Many youth find their first experience of worship along with thousands of peers to be a life-transforming experience. Some conferences even provide on-site opportunities for street evangelism or community service with the aim of sharing God's love.[3]

I once took a few nervous high schoolers to an evangelism training event that focused primarily on helping them build confidence in telling their own faith stories and inviting others to become Christians. While not all of them had a chance to lead someone else to faith personally, the event created an enthusiasm for seeing their own friends become Christians—an enthusiasm that lasted long after we returned. Several parents expressed their appreciation to me. They were excited to see their own kids excited about God—and it made them excited, too.

I was on the "prayer team," a similar event, this time in New York City. My only job was to be in Bryant Park praying while the students, in groups of three, approached and sought to engage people in a conversation, eventually about spiritual things. I noticed one group of students talking with a woman and her two children, who appeared to be about 10 and 12. They talked for 90 minutes (!) and when it came time to part, there were hugs all around.

I later found out that the woman told these young people that her life was a wreck, and she was wondering how she could know God better. Our three conference teenagers were able to answer her questions and pray with her and her kids, a prayer of conversion. With tears in her eyes, she told our teenagers that she had an older son by a previous marriage. Much to their surprise, she pulled out her cell phone, got her 21-year-old son on the line, and told him through her tears, "I've just heard the very best news of my entire life, and I want you to hear it, too!" With that she handed the phone to one of our conference kids! I'm sure you won't be surprised to hear that this story electrified the rest of the conference attendees when it was told that night, as well as parents and leaders back home.

Of course, people can argue against the appropriateness, culturally and theologically, of "cold turkey" evangelism. Though we may come down on the "negative" side, we have to admit that God is capable of arranging what can only be called divine appointments. These appointments can have huge impacts on the kids on the giving end as well as the receiving end.

As a rule, I prefer motivating youth, parents, and other church adults toward outreach efforts in which the prime movers are the church youth themselves. Parents and church leaders want their kids to be excited about God; they want their kids to see God do things only he can do. I'm not a big fan of outreach events where kids bring friends to hear an adult evangelist—but, of course, I admit God can use this approach, too.[4]

Reaching the lost without frustrating the found is an important aspect of youth ministry, even in churches that are already wide open and enthusiastic about outreach. When we balance care for the youth inside our churches with efforts to reach those on the outside, we are far less likely to be fired or experience burnout in our ministries.

As we've seen in this chapter, the evangelism approaches I tend to favor place a lot of emphasis on empowerment, particularly of the youth themselves. But outreach isn't the only arena where empowerment is critical. In the next chapter, we'll look at some other ways in which empowerment can help our ministries soar.

## CHAPTER 10

# EMPOWERMENT

He just wanted to spend time with teens and let them
know they were loved. That's good, and all, but there was
no structure, no schedule, no way for others to volunteer,
nothing the teens themselves could even count on.

The last straw for Pastor Eric's ministry came when the
youths hosted a church dinner and Eric forgot to have
anyone cook. No kidding!

Shannon started out great as our youth pastor, but the
group grew beyond her ability to manage; it all collapsed
around her. She left a broken person.

Rubin left others in charge of an event, but forgot to inform
them of that fact. Kids arrived, no adults.

Incompetent in what areas? All.

One way to soar rather than just survive in youth ministry is to learn about empowerment. You'll find lots of books on the topic of empowerment in the business and self-improvement sections of your typical Barnes & Noble. In youth ministry we can see the importance of empowerment skills in at least three areas: self-empowerment skills, youth empowerment skills, and volunteer empowerment skills. I've made some pretty spectacular mistakes in all three!

# SELF-EMPOWERMENT

I used to be an expert at procrastination. My mental justification for my "just in time" approach to life was that, well, I ultimately did get things done, and I had wonderful ability, it seemed to me, to focus intensely as a true deadline neared. I even felt a sense of God's presence (and mercy?) as I was able to pull off huge projects at the last minute, just in time to avoid personal or academic catastrophe. I liked the adrenaline rush that came with the big push at the end. The "just in time" lifestyle seemed pretty adequate for me as a college student—and even as a seminary student.

When I became a youth pastor, however, I found myself getting caught short. There were the small things like finding a note on the photocopier saying, "repair man has been called" when I ran in to make copies of something just before youth group or Sunday school. Or the late afternoon times when I was ready to open my Bible to begin preparing the study I was to lead that evening and the phone would ring with a kid in true crisis on the other end. Also, I found that the calendar was becoming my enemy—the church board wanted my annual youth budget for the upcoming year turned in by October. The church secretary wanted information for the next month's church calendar by the 20th and seemed to always need info from me for the church newsletter *yesterday*. I found the youth pastor world very different from the student world. As a student, I seemed in control (yes, I had assignments, but I controlled my time), but as a youth pastor, others had some claim to what had once been mine alone. Big transition!

My first retreats were textbook examples of last-minute procrastination. The day before the retreat (and often the day of the retreat) I was finishing my talks, arranging transportation, *shopping for the groceries*, and even calling kids to see if they were coming. By this time I was married, but I didn't realize how hard I was to live with when I was in panic mode as retreats and other youth ministry biggies approached. Finally, just a few hours before another of my scrambling departures for a retreat, my wife burst into tears and sobbed, "We can't go on like this!"

Note to self: When spouse is crying and it's my fault, put down clipboard and duffle bag, push "pause," and consider the error of my ways.

Of course, there are a number of books entirely devoted to being organized in youth ministry. (My favorite is *Youth Ministry Management Tools* by Ginny Olson, Dave Elliot, and Mike Work.) But when it comes to personal organization and self-empowerment, the most important things I've learned can be counted on one hand.

*1. Relaxing in God's Power.* It didn't take me long to realize that I couldn't call my youth to a daily and deep walk with God unless I was there myself. I couldn't help them grow closer to God than I was. So I made a commitment to increase the amount of time I spent alone with God. At first it was only 15 minutes a morning, but gradually I was able to expand my private time with God.

Something else made a big difference here. I began to think more about how my spiritual life was functioning. Was my walk with God characterized by rest or effort? Was I letting God's power, through the Holy Spirit, work in my life, or was I still relying on my own power and "trying my best to live a good Christian life"? When crunch and crisis occur, what happens to my interior life? *The Normal Christian Life* by Watchman Nee helped me answer these questions. One of Nee's main points is that God isn't nearly as interested in *helping* us as he is in *doing it all*—if we learn what it means to lay aside our own strength and self-effort. As we admit our own weaknesses and inadequacies, then we are ready to be filled and infused with that divine dynamite.

*2. The List/The Calendar.* I live by my weekly list of "Things to Do." On Monday morning I write down everything I should accomplish during the week, including desk work, phone calls, e-mails, and personal appointments. The desk work list always has a few *very* short-term items—such as planning a game for Wednesday night, writing the "Youth Scene" bulletin copy, or preparing for Sunday school. There are always some longer-term items as well. In January, for example, I try to get the summer calendar 75 percent done. January is also the time I draft the September schedule and make facility reservations for the winter retreat that's still more than a year down the line.

Looking at the list, I prioritize the items: first, second, third, and so on. Then...with much internal fanfare...*I draw the line.* Say what? I look at the list, look at what else is happening during the week, and draw the line—usually right around item number ten. If the week is heavy with meetings and appointments, the line might be drawn at seven or eight.

What the line means is this: *I will make almost any sacrifice to finish every item above the line.* It's almost like I tell myself the kingdom of God and his church on earth will collapse if I don't finish the items above the line! Sometimes that commitment has meant my coming back to the office late at night after my children are in bed and working until midnight. Sometimes it's meant coming in at 6:30 a.m. But once I've drawn the line, it means— unless I'm sick or dead—*these items will get done.* Usually, the list above the line gets done without resorting to heroics, but if unexpected time gobblers slide into my week, working on "The List" takes place at odd hours.

> Ministry is a team effort. If you are not in a staff situation where the individual's skills and gifts are honored, cultivated, and supported, you may need to look for a new position before you burn out or lose your job.
>
> (BURNED OUT, EVANGELICAL LUTHERAN, SUBURBAN NEW MEXICO.)

For me the secret of being organized and getting things done is to always include several longer-range items above the line. The first week of January, I may put "order summer Sunday school curriculum" above the line. Sure, it's not really crucial that it happens that week—it could be done in May. But I try to schedule these tasks well in advance, so I never have to scramble at the end.

Early in my ministry I realized there's a rhythm to a typical youth ministry year. I started keeping a 3 x 5 card for each month, and I'd write down the big things that needed to be on my list some week during that month. I compared notes with more experienced youth pastors to see how they managed to stay on top of their work.

Have I always been like this? Of course not! I just learned the hard way (picture my spouse weeping) that it's better to learn how to plan ahead and thus avoid the wild-eyed youth worker syndrome.

3. *Controlling Paper.* Similarly, if we're going to make it in youth ministry, we have to figure out how to control paper—and that includes "electronic paper" such as e-mail.

Have you ever wanted to rent a bulldozer or backhoe to clean off the top of your desk? I sure have. Oh, how nice it would be just to scoop it all up and spill it out the window to an eager dumpster below.

I like files and notebooks. When I was a full-time youth pastor, my notebook for the senior high student leadership team had the following sections: Leader Meetings: Future, Current, and Past; Team Lists; Planning Calendar; and Ideas. My senior high group section in the file cabinet includes files like Current Quarter Wednesdays; Outreach Events: Pending, Current, and Past; Retreats: Pending, Current, and Past; Service Project Ministries; Parent Meetings: Pending, Current, and Past; and Discipleship.

I also have a hanging file folder for each book of the Bible. This is especially helpful since our junior and senior highers are on a six-year curriculum plan. (See Appendix B.) The junior high cycle repeats every two years, and the senior high rolls over every four years. Since I was at one church for 14 years, I was eventually on my fourth time through the cycle with the senior highers. When 1 Timothy came up again, for example, I'd pull that file and see what I'd done the previous time(s). I would make improvements each time.

I have a file drawer of other topics: suicide, sex, peer pressure, and so on. In that same drawer is information from youth organizations: Youth Specialties, Sonlife, Youth for Christ, and so on. Of course broadband Internet means I don't have to keep nearly as much paper information about topics and organizations as I once did. With great joy in my heart, I recently collapsed the contents of a five-drawer file cabinet into a single drawer in another file cabinet and put the emptied one out front with a "free" sign on it.

I have a set of e-files as well and try not to allow more than 15 e-mails to carry over on my screen from the previous day. Dealing with incoming e-mail can be a huge issue. I have a ministry friend who confessed he had over 500 unanswered (non-spam) e-mails. He often encounters people who are disappointed (or angry) that he isn't better at answering.

It doesn't matter how we do it, but we have to do it successfully—manage the (e)paper we create and the stuff that comes in our direction. It's not hard to see how success here helps us in long-term ministry. If my student leadership team wants to do a van rally, I don't have to start from zero. I can go to my "Outreach: Past" file—which is subdivided with separate files on van rallies, scavenger hunts, and similar events. We can choose a van rally done more than four years ago, pull the paper on it, revise it if we want, and go to press.

*4. Personal Preparation.* Preparation style can vary widely, but the bottom line is the same. When it comes to something for which we are responsible, are we ready? Have we worked hard, or do we wing it hard? Have we avoided the "Saturday Night Special Syndrome"? I encourage youth workers to avoid last-minute preparation because Murphy's Law is alive and well— if something can go wrong, it probably will. When things that are prepared in advance come apart, at least we have time to glue them back together.

*5. Following Through and Keeping One's Word.* One final aspect of personal empowerment has to do with returning phone calls and making sure I follow through if I say I'm going to do something. If I say I'm going to call someone or take care of some task, I make sure it gets on my week's list and, by God's grace, it happens. If your word isn't good, the credibility of your ministry will suffer.

# STUDENT EMPOWERMENT

From time to time I have opportunities to visit or speak to other youth groups. Sometimes this experience is a little depressing, because I see a room full of apathetic kids. I remember one especially uncomfortable time when I watched my youth pastor friend plead with his group to grow in God, to care about the youth group, and to care about one another. I didn't see one young person who showed the slightest sign of paying attention or caring about anything other than the person sitting next to them. For my friend, it was one of those "Perhaps I should be working at Home Depot or Wal-Mart after all" moments. His youth felt no ownership of the ministry—it was all being done for them and to them. It doesn't have to be that way.

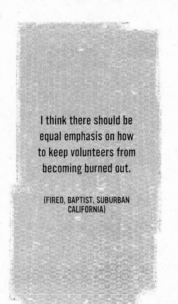

I think there should be equal emphasis on how to keep volunteers from becoming burned out.

(FIRED, BAPTIST, SUBURBAN CALIFORNIA)

It took me years of mistakes to finally come up with some ways to help students feel committed to Christ as well as to the student ministry and the church. Here are a few of my best ideas—some that I adapted from other youth workers, and some I stumbled on myself.

## Recruiting Student Leaders

Get a room full of youth pastors together and there will be no end to opinions on the right approach to recruiting student leaders. Some of my youth pastor friends in New York City have youth leadership elections and elaborate inauguration ceremonies. Some of my friends in California have a leadership team that's entirely voluntary—the youth themselves decide whether they'll serve as leaders and for how long.

I prefer an approach somewhere between these two, in which I take a poll of the group (not a vote) to see who the youth feel could be good student leaders. Near the end of the school year—usually in May—I give everyone a page with the youth in next year's group listed—the guys on one side and the girls on the other. I ask everyone present to circle a few names on each side—the kids they think are 1) most committed to Christ and 2) most committed to this student ministry. I compile the list and then meet with the outgoing seniors (who have been the core of the group), and we prayerfully pick the new leadership team.

After the nominees for the team have been selected, I phone them to ask if they will be on the team. Most are excited to be chosen. I let them know that serving on the leadership team includes an expectation that they'll seek to continue growing spiritually and that they'll regularly attend all youth group events. If they feel ready to join the team, I invite them to a special orientation gathering with the other members of the new leadership team.

That's the process we've used to choose the student leadership team at the churches where I've been a youth pastor. But the longer I do this, the more convinced I am that it doesn't matter so much how we get a leadership team—what matters is what we do once we have one. How we orient leaders and how we meet with them are the keys.

## Orientation That Leads to Ownership and Empowerment

I usually hold the orientation gathering in June—shortly after the new team members are chosen. After a relaxing barbeque or some other informal kind of dinner, preferably in a home or outdoor park, I gather the new leadership team in a circle. Here's what comes next:

1. I affirm my own joy in them and my delight in the last school year. With that intro, I have them go around the circle, each sharing one good student ministry memory from the past year. This usually results in laughter and many smiles as different memories are shared around the circle.

2. Next I affirm that I'm impressed that they are willing to step up to this commitment. I give each of them a sheet titled "RESPONSIBILITIES..." That sheet has four blank sections, with the following headings: "...to God," "...to the Rest of the Leadership Team," "...to the Entire Youth Group," and "...to the Adult Leaders." I have the students divide into four small groups and assign each group one category (e.g. "Responsibility to God"), inviting them to spend a few minutes brainstorming what their responsibilities as student leaders should be in that area. When the full team reconvenes, each small group reports back and, if we all agree on what they've said, we write each item down on our own sheets. I also throw each category open for additional suggestions, but I'm careful to make sure that each idea is affirmed by the whole group.

You'll notice immediately how this approach departs from what is often done. Many youth workers determine for themselves the responsibilities of student leaders and then pronounce these expectations from "on high" a little like Moses speaking to the people of Israel. That is a very top-down approach. I like to let the responsibilities emerge from the leaders themselves, and they agree to them by consensus. I make a big deal out of their agreeing to the responsibilities, because we will hold one another accountable to these commitments in our regular meetings.

3. I hand out our statement of the youth ministry's mission/vision/core values. Most will be quite familiar with this already, but here we affirm that everything we plan must fit into the mission/vision.

4. I hand them a blank calendar for the months of September through December (remember, this is being done in May or June), and we brainstorm possible outreach and service events, fitting them into the calendar in a way that makes sense with other things (like retreats, mission conference, etc.) Be sure to check the church calendar before doing this step—you don't want to have a multi-church Jell-O wrestling exhibition or pudding fight on the same day as a wedding—no matter how hard you try to clean up, it won't satisfy the bride's mother! (Voice of experience speaking!)

5. We close in prayer of thanks for each other and the joy of serving Christ.

# Student Leadership Team Meetings That Empower

Of all the things I've done as a youth pastor, the twice-monthly meeting with the student leadership team has always been among the things I most look forward to. And the students enjoy them, too.

We'd normally gather for 90-120 minutes, sitting on the floor in a circle or on couches. First, we go around the room and share either a "praise" or "prayer" item. We may also throw in an accountability question for each youth to respond to, such as "Share something from your devotional life in the last week" or "Who, in the group, did you speak with since we last met who you don't normally speak with?" If they share a prayer request, it should be a personal one—not a concern about an uncle's cousin's sister-in-law's lost pet. With 10-12 of us present at this meeting, the sharing and prayer may take as much as 45 minutes.

Next we evaluate: "Anyone want to reflect on anything that has happened in the ministry since we last met?"

Third, we plan for the future. In terms of our outreach and service events, we're usually looking four to six months down the line. In my youth ministries over the years, I've usually found it best to have *kids plan* while *adults program*. That is, kids come up with the kinds of events we'll do, but it is the adult staff that takes those plans and carries them out with the assistance of the youth. If we've planned an outreach event, we might go around the circle and answer the question: "Does this event look good enough that you'll eagerly invite a friend?" If the honest answer isn't yes, we work at it some more. (I realize not every youth ministry has "events" other than its main weekly meeting.)

We also plan how members of the student leadership team will be involved in our weekly youth group meetings. Individuals

> Be mindful of how you "fit" into the church. Finding a place where you fit well with the church style, ministry staff relationships, etc., will go a long way in making it a good place to work and minister. Know yourself and who you really are.
>
> (FIRED, NONDENOMINATIONAL, SUBURBAN OHIO)

may lead some aspect of the Bible study, be involved in worship leading, or marketing (skit, media) some event.

A fourth component of the meeting is a ten-minute training module. This usually relates to helping their peers.

Before the meeting ends I throw it open to anything people want to bring up.

Finally—and this is what I really look forward to—we put the chairs in a circle, kneel down in front of them, and pray for the ministry. We prayed for one another at the beginning of the meeting; now we pray for the ministry itself. Sometimes we go into the church sanctuary and kneel there. (I find the junior high leadership team really likes the sanctuary as a place to pray.)

Throughout the first few months of each school year, I have the fun of seeing the hearts of the student leaders change. They once were youth group *consumers*. "What's here for me?" These leadership team meetings change them so they start to ask a different question: "What does God want me to give?"

## One More Idea for Empowering Youth

Here's a rule of thumb I like to use: The larger and more important the event, the more important it is that it be student-led. In fact, I aim to have the most important meetings and events led *entirely* by students—no adults are in front leading or saying anything the entire time. I realize this is not always possible, especially if you're just beginning to build a youth ministry. However, I've seen kids come alive when they really figure out the adults believe in them. And I've seen adult volunteers, who'd never seen kids lead before, sit in wide-eyed, drop-jawed amazement the first time we held an entirely student-led meeting after I became the new youth pastor.

One likely outcome of an emphasis on student leadership will be numerical growth in the student ministry. As I mentioned in the previous chapter, my study of 500 youth ministries around the country found that change in the amount of time kids were up front leading their peers was the single most important variable associated with a ministry's numerical growth.

Yes, growing numbers are exciting. Yet a ministry that empowers students will also be one where the gospel is as much caught as taught and where youth themselves feel they matter to God and the work of his kingdom.

# EMPOWERING ADULT VOLUNTEERS

I'm sorry to say that in my first five years as a youth pastor, I was a true expert at being incompetent when it came to working with volunteers and parents. Being a Lion (see chapter 5), I wasn't very sensitive to signs that all was not well. I didn't pick up on it when people would resign soon after starting as volunteers, or when I'd hear adult leaders talking to each other and saying they had "no idea what's going on." I think the first time I realized we had a problem was when I was hurrying to the youth room with both arms full of sports gear, and a volunteer snidely commented, "Len, don't you even trust us to carry the equipment?"

Ouch.

The real crisis came, however, when a church board member took me to lunch one day. He was also a volunteer on my senior high staff as well as a parent of a junior higher. I still remember exactly what he told me: "I think you're doing a great job working with the youth, Len. You really seem to know what you're doing. Unfortunately, you don't seem to have any idea how to work with adults who want to help out. You'll never last here unless you get this figured out…"

Double ouch.

> Spend your time and money investing in great volunteers and support staff. The ministry must continue, even when you get sick or take a vacation!
>
> (BURNED OUT, ROMAN CATHOLIC, URBAN TEXAS)

He went on to help me see that one aspect of youth ministry was learning different skill sets. I needed certain gifts and skills to work with youth—and I was pretty good at most of those. However, I needed an entirely different skill set to work with adults who work with youth. I was on a steep learning curve, that's for sure, but eventually this aspect of ministry became more of a strength for me than a weakness.

Now I see four important skills that together will help adult volunteers feel empowered and unleashed to serve with enthusiastic joy.

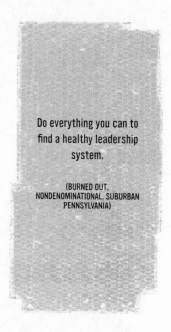

Do everything you can to find a healthy leadership system.

(BURNED OUT, NONDENOMINATIONAL, SUBURBAN PENNSYLVANIA)

## Motivating

As the youth pastor, my job is to encourage, encourage, and encourage some more any volunteers who are part of the ministry. With volunteers, I use a format involving initial orientation and regular meetings similar to what I do with the student leadership team. I get feedback that these meetings are both encouraging and motivating.

I try to have an orientation meeting for all volunteers in late August or early September. In addition to fun, prayer, mission/vision/core values review, and going over job descriptions (see below), I give the "Lion, Otter, Golden Retriever, Ant" personality test to make sure everyone has a good feel of the strengths and passions of the others.

Our volunteers commit to a monthly evening gathering that is for them. The meetings are usually held at someone's home, and the normal components include:

1. A meal.

2. Prayer for one another. (As with the student leaders, personal requests only.)

3. Evaluation/reflection on the month that's past since our last meeting.

4. Programming. We take the plan of the student leaders and designate which adults will be "in charge" of each event. (Keep personality types in mind: Lions are just waiting to be asked to lead,

while Golden Retrievers prefer not to be up front or in charge.) We talk through the schedule and any specifics that help make sure we have all the bases covered.

5. Training. We usually talk through a copied article on youth ministry from *Youthworker, Group,* or *Journal of Student Ministries.* Some years we've read through a book on youth ministry together, discussing a chapter at each meeting.

6. Talk about specific kids or specific situations. Any concerns? Anyone needing special care?

7. Prayer for the ministry. If the setting is conducive, we do so on our knees.

## Visualizing

Another key in empowering others in youth ministry is being able to visualize exactly what we want our youth staff and volunteers to do. What, really, do we want the adults working with us to do? If your answer is, "Come and watch me do what I'm good at while you sit around with kids," it's the wrong answer! Everyone likes to feel successful, right? How will they know when they are succeeding?

Once we have an idea of what we want volunteers to do, we need to write it down. Yes, I realize it's not very postmodern, but people actually like to have clarity if they are going to volunteer their time. Time is what many people feel they lack most, so they want their volunteer time to matter. I find writing job descriptions helps me clarify for myself what needs to be done, and it helps our adult leaders know what is expected.

Here's a job description for adults working with our senior high youth ministry that I've used in two churches as youth pastor.

## Senior High Ministry Team Member

### FUNCTION

To be used by the Lord in the lives of senior high young people. To love, encourage, and become closely involved with them. To do everything possible to make our ministry with senior high youth excellent.

### RESPONSIBILITIES

#### 1. FOR YOUR MINISTRY

* To attend Wednesday night youth group regularly. To attend other events on a rotating basis.
* To build relationships with the youth on your team, working closely with team leaders.
* To have informal contacts with the youth on your team outside of youth group night.
* To help lead your team in the context of the youth group meeting (small group discussions, prayer, etc.)

#### 2. FOR YOUR OWN GROWTH

* To have a consistent and quality devotional life, growing more and more in love with Christ.
* To attend ministry team meetings on a monthly basis.
* To read one book on youth ministry during the year or attend one special training event.

#### 3. YOU'LL KNOW YOU'RE SUCCEEDING WHEN:

* You know the names of the youth and something about them and their families.
* You feel comfortable talking with them informally.
* You can lead a discussion or prayer time with your team.
* Kids come up to you to say "hi" or just to talk.
* You know them well enough so they know you care and are willing to share below-the-surface things going on in their lives.

* You occasionally carve out time outside of youth group night to contact or be with them.

## TERM OF SERVICE

One school year. Everyone is "fired" in June but is welcome to come back for the next school year. You are expected to take the summer off. (A summer-only staff is recruited to give you the time off.) Your "job" is to come back refreshed!

## Scheduling/Communicating

I learned (again, the hard way) that once I wasn't the only adult working with the youth, I had to learn how to think ahead. It wasn't any good to call my already-busy volunteers at the last minute (or even the week before) and ask them to attend or help with something extra. This forced me to plan, in advance, with the student leadership team, so I could come to the adult volunteers with what was going on far enough in advance that it was easy to have volunteers help in various ways. There were tasks I used to do myself at the last minute, but finally I learned that others enjoyed helping in specific ways—like coordinating transportation to an off-site event, or recruiting parents to provide refreshments, or making sure all the equipment is handy for a series of games, or being in charge of the media equipment.

According to my volunteers over the years, the single most helpful piece of paper I've ever given them is a simple "Who's Doing What" flow sheet. I gave them one for the regular youth group meetings (including three months' worth of meetings) and another for the schedule of outreach or service events (also three months at a time). The sheets are simple:

For each event: date, time, name of event, who has agreed to be "in charge."

For weekly youth group meetings: date, text/topic, worship leader, main teacher, main "up front" person. (Whenever possible, the worship leader, main teacher, and main up front person were students.)

At our monthly volunteer staff meeting, we would work through the "Who's Doing What" sheets, filling in any and all blank spaces.

I realize that the programming for some youth ministries usually involves a weekly meeting that has essentially the same components led by the same person or persons each week. Many other youth ministries, however, build upon this basic weekly meeting and have additional ministry components. My "planning cycle"— again, learned over a long period of time after a lot of failure— looks something like this:

JUNE: Work on September–December

OCTOBER: Work on January–March

JANUARY: Work on April–June

APRIL: Work on July–August.

Here, "work on" involves a three-step process:

1. Student Leadership Team makes the plans.

2. I develop the "Who's Doing What" flow sheet.

3. I work through the flow sheet with the volunteer staff.

Of course certain events and projects require a longer-term time frame. For example, in the places I've ministered, scheduling ice time (at a rink) for broomball has to be done six months in advance. If I wait until October to try to get ice time in January, I won't find any time that's available. Another example is when planning something with one or more youth groups from other churches. Spontaneity rarely works in such situations. They must be planned months in advance.

Could I do this kind of advance planning in my first couple of years in youth ministry? Of course not—I was too consumed with the immediate details. Eventually, though, it just made sense to think further ahead. This helped my volunteers get youth ministry commitments on their own schedules and give them priority.

We've spent many chapters building fences against failure and burnout. We've explored ideas and insights that may even help us soar. We conclude with the notion that the Lord is in the business of restoration and renewal—specifically...with us!

# CHAPTER 11

# THE RENEWED YOUTH WORKER

I was physically and emotionally exhausted. For a variety of reasons, our backpacking trip to the Whistler Peak area had turned sour. Normally these adventure trips were a joy to lead and a completely positive experience for the senior highers who attended. But this year, by the third day, I was just tired—tired of kids complaining and sometimes being uncooperative, tired of crummy weather, tired of overzealous park rangers, tired of trying to keep a pair of hormone-stricken teens from sneaking into each other's sleeping bags in the middle of the night. So on the fourth morning of the trip, when a couple of macho seniors told me they wanted to do some cliff jumping into the lake, I didn't lift a finger in protest. Yes, 50 feet is a steep jump, but the water was deep. No problem.

Actually, it was a problem. The macho guys who'd approached me with the idea were fine, but a couple of other students who'd tried to join in on the fun got injured—one of them requiring medical evacuation. I faced my own feelings of guilt and remorse for letting things get out of control. And I knew I'd soon be facing the wrath of some of the parents back at church for allowing a clearly unsafe activity to occur.

But I recovered. Then, as in many times before and since, I found that God is in the restoration business. He is all about extreme makeovers. When I am brought low through my own sin, poor judgment, or both, God meets me in my pain, offering grace and hope.

I've come to lean on Isaiah 40:31:

> But those who hope in the Lord will renew their strength. They will soar on wings like eagles; they will run and not grow weary, they will walk and not be faint.

This verse causes me to think of youth ministry in three modes: *soaring* (when everything is going amazingly great and I feel fully alive), *running* (when everything is fine and I feel good, even as I encounter the normal speed bumps of life and ministry), and *walking*, which I would restate as *crawling* (when the skies have turned dark, and crises knock me low).

I'm sure just about every long-term youth pastor has her or his own list of what makes it possible to get through the hard times, what it is that makes renewal happen so that we can survive the *crawling* times without grinding to a complete halt and get back to *running* or *soaring*. My own list is implied throughout this book. Here are a few final additions to that list to help keep you strong for the journey ahead.

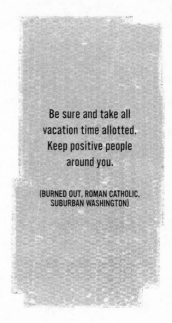

Be sure and take all vacation time allotted. Keep positive people around you.

(BURNED OUT, ROMAN CATHOLIC, SUBURBAN WASHINGTON)

## DRAW BOUNDARIES

Archibald Hart in his book, *Adrenaline and Stress,* explains how important it is for the human body to have times when adrenaline is not being dumped into the bloodstream. In a typical day of ministry, our adrenal glands work hard much of the time. When we come home, be it a country house on the farm or a two-room apartment in the Bronx, we need to let our adrenaline level come down.

One problem about home, and really wherever we are when we are "off," is that we're often still *connected*. We can be doing our own fun Web searches and—boom, someone IMs us. If we want to take care of our bodies, we've got to learn to disconnect, to draw a boundary. Hart explains some in ministry are so addicted to adrenaline that finally the body's immune system collapses (think mono or worse) and they are forced to stop. It's not healthy for us (or our ministries) if we are on call 24/7/365. We need time away. Going for very long without a Sabbath carries huge risks for our emotional, spiritual, and physical health.

> I don't think a lot of ministry people are very good at taking care of their own souls—they are so focused on the souls of others. Get spiritual nourishing, have a mentor.
>
> (BURNED OUT, PRESBYTERIAN, SUBURBAN CALIFORNIA

## DEVELOP A HEALTHY VULNERABILITY

None of us is perfect. We are all just plain human beings, and we have problems. Others can help minister to our needs, if we are willing and able to share them appropriately.

Of course, wisdom means knowing what to share with whom. If your problem is lust, perhaps you'd better not mention that in your junior high Bible study. Hate your senior pastor? Don't lay that burden on your volunteer staff. My wife and I are in a small group with three other couples. Within that group, pretty much anything can be said in confidence, and we can receive the comfort, help, and support of the body of Christ up close. I also have a male friend who is my accountability partner. We share deeply with each other about what's going on our lives, and keep each other on a short leash when it comes to moral choices.

# NEVER FORGET THE KINGDOM OF GOD WILL ALWAYS GO ON

Continued renewal is possible in our lives when we remember the big picture. My lake-jumping catastrophe did not bring the kingdom of God crashing down. Nor did my outreach-concert disaster where income came $6000 short of expenses and no one "came forward." The kingdom wasn't destroyed when I had to threaten to expel Troy, the "troubled" eighth-grade boy who used to really enjoy shocking everyone by simulating having sex with a particular couch in our youth group room (not sex *on* the couch, but sex *with* the couch). The hyperactive girl in my current junior high group who likes to impersonate demons can be a real problem—but this too will pass.

In youth ministry over the years, I've managed to make most of the people happy most of the time. But I've also learned that, sure enough, the work of God goes on around the world even if Mrs. Weasel feels I'm not doing my job right. It's important that I make sure I'm being sensitive to the needs of the Mrs. Weasels in my church, but if I fail from time to time, it seems the kingdom manages to lurch ahead anyhow.

Honest connecting with others in the field that focuses on Bible study and helping voice concerns and challenges is essential. It's also good when the church has a staff or personnel committee whose job it is to actually care for the paid staff.

(BURNED OUT, LUTHERAN MISSOURI SYNOD, SUBURBAN FLORIDA)

# DON'T NEGLECT THE INNER LIFE

I know you know that we, as youth workers, have to dwell deeply in Christ. If we ignore our inner life, we don't have a prayer.

We face a myriad of obstacles to this deeper walk. There are kids to see, parents to please, retreats to organize, reports to write, and meetings to lead. These are all important parts of any youth ministry, to be sure. But if we are not grounded in Christ, our efforts to do these tasks effectively will fall short. The reality is that the kids we work with may be hard to love; they may be aloof, rude, and seemingly content

> Make sure your own personal spiritual life is on track. You must keep your cup full of God first so that then you can keep giving. If all you do is keep giving, and it never gets refilled from God, you will eventually empty out and burn out.
>
> (BURNED OUT, EVANGELICAL FREE, URBAN NEBRASKA)

with being selfish pigs. Instead of being supportive, the parents may complain to our face. Our senior pastor may be so insecure that he or she speaks against us at board meetings. Our spouse may be frustrated that we always seem to be working or that our income is limited. We may look in vain for a sector of our universe in which we can rest and find comfort...

That's the way it is sometimes in youth work. And you know, that's okay. Multiple troubles, which yank our rugs of security out from under us, force us to look to God.

The prophet Isaiah reminds us of God's present comfort when hard times come. These words, spoken first to Israel, are extended to us as well. This is God talking to you...and these are words of hope, encouragement, and renewal.

> But now, this is what the Lord says—he who created you, Jacob, he who formed you, Israel: "Do not fear, for I have redeemed you; I have summoned you by name; you are mine. When you pass through the waters, I will be with you; and when you pass through the rivers, they will not sweep over you. When you walk through the fire, you will not be burned; the flames will not set you ablaze...You are precious and honored in my sight...I love you." (Isaiah 43:1-2, 4)

Whether we sense it in the depths of our hearts during prayer or feel it in the hug of a caring friend, God's love floods in to refresh a soul that has been baked dry in the oven of ministry trouble.

We must admit our weakness daily and affirm our wish to co-operate with God's desire to live through us. As we do so, we gain the strength to keep going—not only to walk without stumbling or fainting but also to soar like eagles. By opening our hearts, we receive the gift of God's continual renewal, feeding our spirits and empowering us to do youth ministry now and in the years to come.

# APPENDIX A

# RESULTS FROM THE SURVEY OF FIRED OR BURNED-OUT YOUTH PASTORS

This survey of youth ministers who left their jobs due to burnout or being fired was released in early fall 2006. Invitations to participate in the survey were sent to all the youth pastors of two evangelical Protestant denominations, as well as to various other contacts the author had, including members of the Association of Youth Ministry Educators and members of the International Association of Youth Ministry Educators who had filled out a previous international church-based youth ministry survey. The author also made personal contacts with Roman Catholic youth pastors and Diocesan youth ministry coordinators. Respondents could fill out the survey about themselves or someone they knew well.

Anonymity was assured, though there were several questions that provided the author with the ability to cross-check to determine if multiple people were responding about the same person. This cross-checking revealed that less than 1 percent of the 373 responses were duplicates. In the end, none of the duplicate responses were eliminated from the tally for two reasons: 1) Narrative (open-ended) questions provided multiple perspectives on the duplicate cases; and 2) the total number of duplicates was so small that it would not greatly affect statistical results.

The survey was Web-based. Persons received e-mail invitations to participate and had only to click on the URL link to be taken directly to the survey. When participants pushed "submit" after completing the survey, their results were added to the cumulative statistics. There were no "mandatory" questions, so some questions were left unanswered by respondents.

The survey appears below, along with the statistical results. The wording of the questions is exactly as seen by respondents.

## Survey of "Fired" or "Burned-Out" Youth Pastors

1. Initials of fired or burned-out person. (This is to preclude duplicates from other respondents.)

   TOTAL RESPONSES:                         370

2. Continent of residence at the time: (Again to avoid duplications.)

   |                        | PERCENTAGE | RESPONSE TOTAL |
   |------------------------|------------|----------------|
   | North America          | 94.9%      | 354            |
   | South/Central Amer.    | 0          | 0              |
   | Africa                 | .5%        | 2              |
   | Europe                 | 1.9%       | 7              |
   | Asia                   | .5%        | 2              |
   | Australia/New Zealand  | 2.1%       | 8              |
   | TOTAL RESPONSES:       |            | 373            |

3. State or province of residence if within North America, or country if not from the US or Canada. (One last time, to avoid duplications.)

   TOTAL RESPONSES:                         373

4. Sex

   | Male   | 76.5% | 284 |
   |--------|-------|-----|
   | Female | 23.5% | 87  |
   | TOTAL RESPONSES: |  | 371 |

5. Married?

| | | |
|---|---|---|
| Yes | 75.5% | 280 |
| No | 24.5% | 91 |
| TOTAL RESPONSES: | | 371 |

6. College/University graduate

| | | |
|---|---|---|
| Yes | 83.7% | 309 |
| No | 16.3% | 60 |
| TOTAL RESPONSES: | | 369 |

7. Youth Ministry degree from either college or seminary?

| | | |
|---|---|---|
| Yes | 49.2% | 180 |
| No | 50.8% | 186 |
| TOTAL RESPONSES: | | 366 |

8. Length of his/her ministry at the church: (express in terms of years...e.g. 5.2)

| | |
|---|---|
| Average length: | 4.8 years |
| TOTAL RESPONSES: | 372 |

9. The church was in what setting?

| | | |
|---|---|---|
| Urban | 14.5% | 54 |
| Suburban | 61.9% | 231 |
| Rural | 23.6% | 88 |
| TOTAL RESPONSES: | | 373 |

10. The church from which this departure took place was:

Protestant                94.3%              345

Roman Catholic            5.7%               21

11. The personality of the "fired" or "burned-out" person: LION: decisive, natural leader; OTTER: outgoing, spontaneous; GOLDEN RETRIEVER: deeply caring and empathetic; ANT: detailed, very organized and busy. Of course, most people are a combination, but here, choose the ONE main style.

Lion                      24.6%              91

Otter                     32.2%              119

Golden Retriever          30.0%              111

Ant                       13.2%              49

TOTAL RESPONSES:                             370

12. This person was...Fired? Questions 12, 13, ONLY. Burned Out? Skip to Question 14. In either case, check up to three that apply, and you'll be given a chance to elaborate soon.

Church could no longer
afford salary             13.3%              31

Conflict with senior pastor
(over what?)              48.9%              114

Conflict with other church leadership
(over what?)              45.9%              107

Conflict with parents
(over what?)              15%                35

Conflict with kids
(over what)               3.9%               9

| | | |
|---|---|---|
| Sexual impropriety | 6.4% | 15 |
| Money mishandling | 1.7% | 4 |
| Incompetence (elaborate below) | 7.7% | 18 |
| Addiction (to what?) | 0.9% | 2 |
| Philosophy of ministry difference | 33.9% | 79 |
| Other (specify below) | 17.6% | 41 |
| TOTAL PERSONS RESPONDING: | | 233 |

13. Here's your chance to elaborate on any of the above. Tell the story. (No names or specific identities.)

   TOTAL RESPONSES: 219

14. Burned Out? Choose up to four from responses below. (Remember, do NOT answer this if you answered Question 12.)

| | | |
|---|---|---|
| Feelings of personal inadequacy | 23.2% | 36 |
| Too much criticism | 35.5% | 55 |
| Growing loss of confidence | 25.2% | 39 |
| Strained family relations (e.g., not enough time) | 36.1% | 56 |
| Feelings of personal disorganization | 16.8% | 26 |
| Grew weary of spending time with youth | 14.2% | 22 |
| Financial pressures | 25.8% | 40 |
| Spiritual dryness, an unnourished soul | 38.7% | 60 |

| | | |
|---|---|---|
| Pastor hard to get along with | 42.2% | 67 |
| Felt isolated or lonely | 43.2% | 67 |
| Other (specify below) | 29.7% | 46 |
| TOTAL PERSONS RESPONDING: | | 155 |

15. Please elaborate on at least one of the items listed in Question 14. (No names or specific identities.)

TOTAL RESPONSES:                          134

16. If you have some thoughts on how youth pastors can avoid burnout, or getting fired, share them here.

TOTAL RESPONSES:                          248

17. If you checked "Protestant" in Question 10, please state the denomination of the church he/she was serving.

TOTAL RESPONSES:                          333

Denominations representing 5 percent or more of total response:

| | |
|---|---|
| Baptist | 20% |
| Nondenominational | 14% |
| Evangelical Free | 10% |
| Methodist | 9% |
| Lutheran | 8% |
| Charismatic | 8% |
| Presbyterian | 7% |
| Christian & Missionary Al. | 5% |

18. Optional: If you have filled out this survey about YOURSELF, your story may be a real help to other youth workers. The researcher is looking for those willing to write up their stories (1-3 pages) for possible inclusion in his new Youth Specialties/Zondervan book. If interested, supply your name/e-mail address here. (Your name/e-mail will be kept confidential.)

TOTAL RESPONSES:                                    139

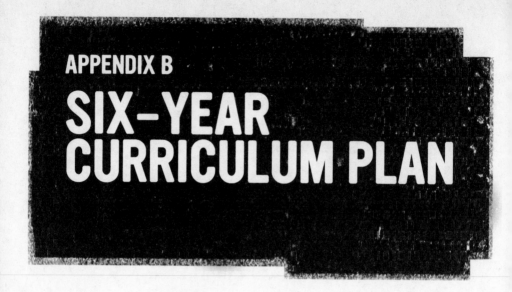

APPENDIX B

# SIX-YEAR CURRICULUM PLAN

## JUNIOR AND SENIOR HIGH MIDWEEK MINISTRIES

### Junior High, Year One

| | |
|---|---|
| Fall | Philippians |
| Winter | Topics |
| Spring | 1 & 2 Peter |
| Summer | Old Testament People |

### Junior High, Year Two

| | |
|---|---|
| Fall | Romans 12-16 |
| Winter | Topics |
| Spring | 1 & 2 Thessalonians |
| Summer | Proverbs |

## Senior High, Year One

Fall         James

Winter       Topics

Spring       1 & 2 Corinthians

Summer       1 & 2 Samuel

## Senior High, Year Two

Fall         Romans 1-8

Winter       Topics

Spring       Romans 12-16

Summer       Psalms

## Senior High, Year Three

Fall         Matthew 5-7

Winter       Topics

Spring       Hebrews

Summer       Genesis

## Senior High, Year Four

Fall         1 & 2 Timothy

Winter       Topics

Spring       Ephesians

Summer       Amos

Note: (a) Gospels are part of the Sunday morning curriculum; (b) Every verse or every paragraph in the listed Bible books is not necessarily covered. The focus may be placed on those verses or sections most relevant to young people; (c) The Winter semester of each year is devoted to topics of special interest; (d) Romans 12-16 is a focus in year two of both the junior-high and senior-high programs. Senior highers are at a different developmental stage from junior highers, so they will "hear" this crucial section in an entirely new way.

# ENDNOTES

## Chapter 1

1. The figure was 4.7 years in a study by Jonathon Grenz "Factors Influencing Vocational Changes Among Youth Ministers," *Journal of Youth Ministry*, Vol. 1, no. 1 (Fall 2002). The figure of 4.2 years came from Gregg Makin's (unpublished) Ph.D. dissertation for Regent University, "Understanding the Turnover Intentions of Youth Pastors," in which he studied 300 members of the National Network of Youth Ministry members. S. Merriman, in doing research for *Group* magazine's (November 2003) biannual youth pastor salary survey offered a figure of 4.8 years. (See groupmag.com.) My own (unpublished) Ph.D. dissertation (Fordham University, 1999) of over 500 youth pastors in four Protestant denominations gave the figure as 3.7 years.

2. Barna Research gives the figure at 5.7 years. http://www.barna.org/FlexPage.aspx?Page=BarnaUpdate&BarnaUpdateID=98

3. Grenz's research, cited above, shows the youth ministry side, as does Strommen/Jones/Rahn. For the pastoral ministry side, the best recent resource is by Dean R. Hogue and Jacqueline Wenger, *Pastors in Transition* (Grand Rapids: Eerdmans, 2005).

4. At least two organizations track youth pastor salaries regularly. Church Law Today publishes an annual *Compensation Handbook for Church*

*Staff* that includes a geographically and denominationally representative annual survey for a variety of church staff positions. It is available from www.churchlawtoday.com. *Group* magazine publishes a report on youth ministry salaries every two years, in its November issue.

5. The National Study of Youth and Religion's Web site contains a literature review section describing over 600 academic studies that have found a correlation between religious faith among youth and pro-social behavior or "assets." See http://www.youthandreligion.org/resources/bibliography.html. The studies cited in the succeeding notes are only a tiny sampling of the academic data on the subject of religiosity and life outcomes among young people.

6. J. Neeleman and G. Lewis, "Suicide, Religion, and Socioeconomic Conditions. An Ecological Study in 26 Countries," *Journal of Epidemiology & Community Health* 53 (1999): 204-210.

7. V. Murrey, "Black Adolescent Females: A Comparison of Early Versus Late Coital Initiators," *Family Relations* 43 (1994): 342-348.

8. John Cochran, "The Effects of Religiosity on Adolescent Self-Reported Frequency of Drug and Alcohol Use," *Journal of Drug Issues* 22 (1992): 91-104.

9. B. Benda and R. Corwin, "Are the Effects of Religion on Crime Mediated, Moderated, and Misrepresented by Inappropriate Measures?" *Journal of Social Service Research* 27 (2001): 57-86.

10. Mark Regnerus, "Shaping Schooling Success: Religious Socialization and Educational Outcomes in Metropolitan Public Schools," *Journal for the Scientific Study of Religion* 39 (2000): 363-370.

11. John Wallace and Tyrone Forman, "Religion's Role in Promoting Health and Reducing Risk Among American Youth," *Health Education and Behavior* 25 (1998): 721-741.

12. Peter Benson, *Troubled Journey: A Portrait of 6th-12th Grade Youth*, (Minneapolis: Search Institute, 1993).

13. Elizabeth Smith, "The Effects of Investments in the Social Capital of Youth on Political and Civic Behavior in Young Adulthood: A Longitudinal Analysis," *Political Psychology* 20 (1999): 553-580.

14. The quote is from an address given by Dr. Leslie Frances of the University of Wales at an Oxford University conference in 1995. His findings were first published in the popular press under the title *Fast Moving Currents in Youth Culture* (Oxford: Lynx Communication, 1995).

15. Christian Smith and Melinda Lundquist Denton, *Soul Searching* (New York: Oxford University Press, 2005).

16. R. Fehring, et al., "Religiosity and Sexual Activity Among Older Adolescents," *Journal of Religion and Health* 37 no. 3 (1998): 229.

17. L. Nicholas, "The Association Between Religiosity, Sexual Fantasy, Participation in Sexual Acts, Sexual Enjoyment, Exposure and Reaction to Sexual Materials Among Black South African Youth," *Journal of Sex & Marital Therapy* 30 (2004): 37-42.

18. I. Sutherland and J. Shepherd, "Social Dimensions of Adolescent Substance Abuse," *Addiction* 96 (2001): 445-458.

19. B. Piko and K. Fitzpatrick, "Substance Use, Religiosity, and Other Protective Factors Among Hungarian Adolescents," *Addictive Behavior* 29, no. 6 (2004): 1095-1107.

## Chapter 2

1. Adapted from notes taken at a Fred Pryor "Leadership Skills" seminar in Seattle, Washington, April 18, 1981. For further information contact Fred Pryor Seminars at www.Pryor.com.

2. The average U.S. adult gains more than a pound each year during his or her entire life. For more information, see www.dietdetectives.com.

3. There are a number of good resources for further information on SAD. You can access the October 2005 *Scientific American* piece at http://www. sciammind.com/article.cfm?articleID=000241B3-2975-132F-A8CA83414B7F0000&pageNumber=4. The Web site of the international Seasonal Affective Disorder Association (headquartered in the UK) receives nearly 1000 hits a day. http://www.sada.org.uk/. A good general information piece on the subject can be had at: http://en.wikipedia.org/wiki/Seasonal_affective_disorder. See also Fiona Marshall and Peter Cheevers, *Positive Options for Seasonal Affective Disorder: Self-Help and Treatment* (Alameda, CA: Hunter House Publishers, 2003).

4. "Sizing Up SADness According to Latitude," *Science News* 136 (September 1989) 198. For a more recent treatment of SAD and latitude see: http://www.ncpamd.com/seasonal.htm#Epidemiology%20of%20SAD

## Chapter 3

1. James Dobson, *Parenting Isn't for Cowards* (Waco, TX: Word, 1987), 36.

## Chapter 4

1. Marcus Buckingham and Curt Coffman, *First, Break All the Rules* (New York: Simon & Schuster, 1999).

2. Paul Borthwick, *Feeding Your Forgotten Soul* (Grand Rapids: Zondervan, 1990).

## Chapter 5

1. This personality type framework was first published by Smalley and Trent in their book on marriage, *The Two Sides of Love* (Carol Stream, IL: Tyndale, 2006). I have changed their original term "Beaver" to "Ant," since the former term

is slang in some countries for something not spoken of in polite society. Information can easily be found by typing the words "Lion, Otter, Golden Retriever..." into most Internet search engines.

2. The subject of the scientific/algorithmic formulas of computer-based personality/compatibility testing services received a major and generally positive review in the March 2006 issue of *Atlantic Monthly* 297, no. 2.

3. Jerome Kagan, with Nancy Snidman, Doreen Arcus, and J. Steven Reznick, *Galen's Prophecy: Temperament in Human Nature* (Boulder, CO: Westview Press, 1995).

4. Daniel Goldman, *Emotional Intelligence: Why It Can Matter More Than IQ* (New York: Bantam, 1995).

## Chapter 6

1. Anonymous, "Why I Left My Husband," *Youthworker* 3, no. 4 (Winter, 1987): 63.

2. Merton Strommen, Karen Jones, Dave Rahn, *Youth Ministry That Transforms* (Grand Rapids, Zondervan, 2001), 93.

3. Steven Nock and Brad Wilcox. *What's Love Got To Do With It? Equality, Equity, Commitment, and Women's Marital Quality.* Available in digital form from Amazon.com. See also the interview with Brad Wilcox in *Christianity Today* www.christianitytoday.com/ct/2006/october/53.122.html.

4. Willard Harley Jr., *His Needs Her Needs* (Grand Rapids: Revell, 1994).

5. For an excellent review of three major Internet matching sites, see Lori Gottlieb's "How Do I Love Thee?" in *Atlantic Monthly* 297, no. 2 (March 2006): 58-70.

## Chapter 7

1. Anthony Campolo. *Growing Up in America* (Grand Rapids: YS/Zondervan, 1989), 170.

2. Dub Ambrose, "Is It Possible to Team Up with Your Pastor?" *Youthworker* 4, no. 4 (Winter 1988): 50-56.

## Chapter 8

1. This is an oft-discussed topic in the New York media but academic study is showing the problem of sexless marriage to be widespread. For example, see www.selfgrowth.com, or do an Internet search for the words "sexless marriage."

2. "A Conversation with Dr. Merton Strommen, "The Five Cries of Parents," *Youthworker* 2, no.1 (Spring 1985): 51.

3. Paul Thigpen. "Layin' Your (Parental) Burden Down," *Youthworker* 2, no.1 (Spring 1985): 62-68.

## Chapter 9

1. Robert Anderson, *Circle of Influence* (Chicago: Moody, 1991), 168-176.

2. For more information go to www.sonlife.com.

3. Another great mega-conference is the DC/LA event, now presented by Youth Specialties. Go to youthspecialties.com/dcla.

4. For a great discussion of this, see Chris Folmsbee's *A New Kind of Youth Ministry* (Grand Rapids: Zondervan/Youth Specialties, 2006).

*Getting Students to Show Up* will challenge you to rethink your methodology when it comes to outreach. But more than that, it'll show you, step-by-step, how to plan and execute a great outreach event for 10 or even 10,000 students.

Whether you're going for a city-wide shindig or a weekly gathering for your church or a campus, you'll find plenty of tips and tools inside that will ensure your event actually reaches out to your demographic and points them toward Jesus.

**Getting Students to Show Up**
Practical Ideas for Any Outreach Event—from 10 to 10,000
Jonathan McKee
RETAIL $9.99
ISBN 978-0-310-27216-8

Doug Fields, author of *What Matters Most* and a youth ministry survivor for more than 25 years, is giving you permission—no, he's telling you—to say "no" and say it often so you can say "yes" to what's most important. If you want to do more than just survive, if you want to thrive in youth ministry, this may be the most important lesson you'll learn.

**What Matters Most**
When NO is better than Yes
Doug Fields
RETAIL $12.99
ISBN 978-0-310-27327-1

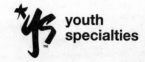

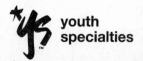

This curriculum course (based on Youth For Christ's 3Story training) offers an interactive learning experience that equips students to live and practice the 3Story way of life—a biblically based, culturally relevant form of discipleship-evangelism. With eight 50-minute training sessions, this curriculum kit is an ideal resource for teaching students how to build deep, authentic relationships with Jesus and genuine, transparent relationships with their friends.

**3Story® Evangelism Training Curriculum**
Preparing Teenagers for a Lifestyle of Evangelism
Youth For Christ
RETAIL $99.99
ISBN 978-0-310-27370-7

visit www.youthspecialties.com/store
or your local Christian bookstore

 youth specialties